At Issue

Greenhouse Gases

Other Books in the At Issue Series:

At Issue

Greenhouse Gases

Ronnie D. Lankford, Jr., Book Editor

GREENHAVEN PRESS
A part of Gale, Cengage Learning

GALE
CENGAGE Learning

Detroit • New York • San Francisco • New Haven, Conn • Waterville, Maine • London

Christine Nasso, *Publisher*
Elizabeth Des Chenes, *Managing Editor*

For more information, contact:
Greenhaven Press
27500 Drake Rd.
Farmington Hills, MI 48331-3535
Or you can visit our Internet site at http://www.gale.cengage.com

For product information and technology assistance, contact us at

Gale Customer Support, 1-800-877-4253
For permission to use material from this text or product, submit all requests online at
www.cengage.com/permissions

Further permissions questions can be emailed to permissionrequest@cengage.com

Articles in Greenhaven Press anthologies are often edited for length to meet page requirements. In addition, original titles of these works are changed to clearly present the main thesis and to explicitly indicate the author's opinion. Every effort is made to ensure that Greenhaven Press accurately reflects the original intent of the authors. Every effort has been made to trace the owners of copyrighted material.

Cover photograph © Images.com/Corbis.

LIBRARY OF CONGRESS CATALOGING-IN-PUBLICATION DATA

Greenhouse gases / Ronnie D. Lankford, Jr., book editor.
       p. cm. -- (At issue)
   Includes bibliographical references and index.
   ISBN-13: 978-0-7377-4100-1 (hardcover)
   ISBN-13: 978-0-7377-4101-8 (pbk.)
 1. Greenhouse gas mitigation. 2. Greenhouse gases. 3. Greenhouse gases
 --Environmental aspects. 4. Global warming. I. Lankford, Ronald D., 1962-
   TD885.5.G73G769 2009
   363.738'74--dc22
                                                      2008026079

Printed in the United States of America
 2 3 4 5 6   13 12 11 10 09

ED119

Contents

Introduction

To understand the current debate surrounding greenhouse gases, it is important to consider the central role of fossil fuels in the economy of the United States. Beginning with the industrial era in the early 1800s, fossil fuel—coal, oil, and natural gas—became the primary energy source in the nation. Use of fossil fuel has only continued to increase, and today the U.S. Department of Energy states that fossil fuel "currently provide[s] more than 85 percent of all the energy consumed in the United States, nearly two-thirds of our electricity, and virtually all of our transportation fuels." As much as some may argue that fossil fuels have improved the American way of life, fossil fuels add carbon dioxide to the Earth's atmosphere, which many claim is harmful. If carbon dioxide adds or causes global warming, as a number of scientists maintain, then reducing Americans' reliance on fossil fuels becomes paramount.

America's Addiction to Fossil Fuel

The lifestyle of most Americans is linked to cheap fossil fuels. For many Americans, however, the depth of this connection remains unclear. Most Americans know that fossil fuels are used in the forms of gasoline to fuel cars and SUVs, and that natural gas is used to heat many homes. But it is perhaps less well known that fossil fuels underpin most of the industrial sector, residential electricity, and agricultural production, and that fossil fuels are essential to the manufacture of many consumer products. Reducing greenhouse gases and replacing fossil fuels is a massive undertaking, and goes well beyond developing more fuel-efficient cars, or turning down the thermostat.

According to *Solcom House*, the United States uses approximately 20.8 million barrels of oil per day. This oil, along with coal and natural gas, accounts for over 85 percent of the energy consumed in the nation. Oil supplies 97 percent of the fuel used for automobiles, and supplies 40 percent of the country's energy consumption. Many everyday products, including glasses, crayons, dishwashing liquids, deodorant, ammonia, and tires, are also made from petroleum. One-half of U.S. homes are heated by natural gas (natural gas accounts for 23 percent of overall energy consumption in the nation); nearly 60 percent of American homes use electricity produced by coal-burning power plants (coal accounts for 22 percent of overall energy consumption in the nation). Maintaining the current level of energy use in the United States requires an average of seven gallons of gasoline per person per day.

Fossil fuels are also essential in agriculture production, which in 2000 accounted for 10 percent of energy usage in the nation. According to *Sustainable Table,* the heaviest use of fossil fuels in the creation of agricultural products is not fuel for farming equipment, but the chemicals used in pesticides and fertilizers. In addition, fossil fuels are required in the packaging and transportation of all agricultural products. "The average American foodstuff," notes *Sustainable Table,* "travels an estimated 1,500 miles before being consumed."

Fossil Fuel Alternatives

Reducing greenhouse gases (specifically carbon dioxide) will require relying less on fossil fuels or learning how to utilize fossil fuels more efficiently. To do this, Americans will have to rely on new technology and alternative fuel sources. Few scientists and environmentalists know with certainty, however, what role these new technologies and fuel sources will play. Furthermore, it is difficult to predict the impact these new technologies will have on the U.S. economy. All that is obvious is that any change will require a massive effort due to the current reliance on fossil fuels.

Corn-based ethanol, one frequently promoted example of a renewable energy resource, highlights the obstacles of replacing fossil fuels with alternative sources. According to *Our Finite World*, 20 percent of the United States's corn crop was converted into ethanol in 2006, accounting for 2.4 percent of the overall gasoline supply. Besides requiring one-fifth of the corn crop to produce a relatively small fuel return, fossil fuels must be used to 1) grow corn, and 2) covert it to ethanol. As a result, critics maintain that the advantage of using ethanol (which, when combined with gasoline, causes petroleum to burn more efficiently) produces little to no net energy gain.

Similar problems may exist with other alternative fuels. In regard to nuclear fission, some scientists have suggested that there is too little uranium to provide a long-term solution. Solar power will require extensive land space for sun collectors or a large number of massive satellites to collect the sun's rays; wind power, collected at distant locations, may require a new kind of power grid. Others have suggested using pure hydrogen extracted by solar or wind power as an energy source, though it is unclear how efficient the process would be.

Changing the Way We Live

While one might guess that scientific disagreement pertaining to the connection between greenhouse gases and global warming has slowed the political response, this is only partially true. A number of regulations have attempted to curb greenhouse gases in the U.S., but as populations have grown, so have carbon dioxide emissions. While environmentalists argue that current regulations are too lenient, another long-term obstacle remains: most factories, power plants, homes, and automobiles are currently designed for the consumption of fossil fuels. Even conversion, however, creates a contradiction: new technology will initially rely on fossil fuels for its creation.

The subject of greenhouse gases has become so contentious because the issue, and what will be done about it, will potentially impact Americans in a profound way. This is not to insist that converting to new fuel sources and technologies is impossible, but to emphasize the United States's current reliance on fossil fuels. The cost of gas at the pump, the cost of one's electric bill, and the cost of groceries at the store are all based on the cost of fossil fuels that create greenhouse gases. To alter the primary fuel source in the United States is to potentially change or alter the way Americans have lived throughout the 20th and the beginning of the 21st centuries.

1

An Overview of Greenhouse Gases

Environmental Literacy Council

The Environmental Literacy Council is dedicated to providing a better understanding of environmental needs.

Greenhouse gases are an important component in maintaining the earth's atmosphere. The gases include water vapor, carbon dioxide, methane, nitrous oxide, ozone, and halocarbons, and occur both naturally and anthropogenically (derived from human activities). Some greenhouse gases remain in the atmosphere longer than others, and the impact of some greenhouse gases— like nitrous oxide—remains mostly unknown. The reaction of various greenhouse gases is complex, and the impact of increased carbon dioxide and methane levels remain heavily debated topics.

Atmospheric greenhouse gases play a critical role in shaping our global climate. Naturally-occurring trace gases in the atmosphere include water vapor, carbon dioxide, methane, nitrous oxide, and ozone. Human activities also impact the concentrations of these gases in the atmosphere. In addition, many commonly used industrial products, including solvents, adhesives, and pesticides, contain halocarbons that can impact the climate. The full range of sources of greenhouses gases— both natural and anthropogenic—is not yet fully understood and continues to be the subject of both research and debate.

Water Vapor

Water vapor is the most abundant of the greenhouse gases, and is the dominant contributor to the natural greenhouse effect. Human activity has little direct impact on the concentration of water vapor in the atmosphere; however, changes in its concentration are an indirect result of climate change and offer feedback related to the warming of the atmosphere.

Carbon dioxide is released into the atmosphere through both natural and human processes.

As temperatures rise, more water evaporates from ground sources—rivers, oceans, etc. Because the air is warmer, the relative humidity can also be higher, leading to more water vapor in the atmosphere. Higher concentrations of water vapor are able to absorb more thermal infrared radiation from the Earth, further warming the atmosphere. The warmer atmosphere can then hold more water vapor, and the cycle continues. This cycle is considered a *positive feedback loop*. However, uncertainty exists in both the extent and importance of this feedback loop. As water vapor increases in the atmosphere, more of it will also condense into clouds, which reflect incoming solar radiation away from the Earth's surface, thereby acting as a cooling force.

Carbon Dioxide

Carbon dioxide is released into the atmosphere through both natural and human processes. Natural production and absorption of carbon dioxide occurs primarily through the biosphere and the oceans via the carbon cycle. Human activities such as fuel burning (coal, oil, natural gas, and wood), cement production, and changes in land use have altered the natural carbon cycle by increasing the concentration of carbon dioxide in the atmosphere.

Carbon dioxide was the first greenhouse gas found to be increasing in atmospheric concentration. Conclusive measurements were made in the last half of the 20th century. Carbon dioxide levels as a component of the atmosphere have increased nearly 30 percent beginning from the late 18th century to the present time, and are now at approximately 370 parts per million (ppm) and rising. Prior to industrialization, carbon dioxide levels fluctuated near 280ppm, with seasonal variations as vegetation drew down carbon dioxide in the spring and summer for photosynthesis, releasing it in the fall and winter through decomposition.

Methane

Methane, which comes from both natural and human sources, is an extremely powerful warming agent—even more effective than carbon dioxide—but its lifetime in the atmosphere is brief, lasting only about 12 years.

In nature, methane is released through biological processes in low oxygen environments, such as swamplands. Human activities, including growing rice, raising cattle, using natural gas, and coal mining, are increasingly adding to the level of methane in the atmosphere. Since the beginning of the 19th century, methane levels have risen 150 percent, though the pattern of methane emissions is highly irregular and, since 1990, has leveled off for reasons that are unclear.

Nitrous Oxide

Nitrous oxide, otherwise known as "laughing gas," is a long-lived warming gas, persisting in the atmosphere for approximately 120 years. It is produced naturally from a wide variety of biological sources in both soil and water, particularly microbial action in wet tropical forests. Human-related sources of nitrous oxide include agricultural soil management, animal manure management, sewage treatment, combustion of fossil fuel, and the production of a variety of acids.

It is also important to account for the various interactions between natural processes and human influences in the nitrogen cycle, since human impacts can significantly enhance the natural processes that lead to N_2O formation. For example, fertilizer use and nitrogen-loaded runoff into waterways can enhance nitrous oxide emissions from natural sources. Concentrations of nitrous oxide began to rise at the beginning of the industrial revolution, although emissions have been somewhat difficult to quantify on a global scale, primarily because it is one of the least studied greenhouse gases to date.

Ozone

Ozone is a highly reactive molecule composed of three atoms of oxygen. Ozone concentrations vary by both geographic location and altitude. At lower levels in the troposphere, ozone exerts a warming force upon the atmosphere, primarily due to human processes. Automobile emissions, industrial pollution, and the burning of vegetation increase the levels of carbon and nitrogen molecules that—when reacting to sunlight— produce ozone, an important contributor to photochemical smog. Levels of ozone have nearly doubled since the 1800s, and have increased nearly 30 percent since the industrial revolution.

In the stratosphere, a decrease in ozone concentration exerts a cooling force upon the atmosphere. Much of the decline in this stratospheric ozone can be attributed to the destructive action of chlorofluorocarbons [CFCs] (see below). As ozone continues to contribute both to the warming and cooling of the atmosphere, its role in the overall enhancement of the greenhouse effect will continue to be difficult to determine.

Halocarbons

Halocarbons are compounds of human origins used primarily as cooling agents, propellants, and cleaning solvents in a broad range of applications. The most familiar type of halocarbons are the chlorofluorocarbons (CFCs); however, since it was discovered that they destroy stratospheric ozone, they are being phased out under the terms of the Montreal Protocol. Although levels of CFCs are declining, their long atmospheric lifetimes assure that they will continue to contribute to the greenhouse effect for some time.

Another set of synthesized halocarbon compounds—created as substitutes to replace CFCs—are called HFCs (hydrofluorcarbons). While they are also greenhouse gases, they are less stable in the atmosphere and therefore have a shorter lifetime and have less of an impact as a greenhouse gas. Also, at lower altitudes, halocarbons function as a warming gas; however, in the upper atmosphere, they exert a cooling impact through their interaction with ozone. Therefore, the ultimate impact of halocarbons on the greenhouse effect is highly uncertain.

2

Greenhouse Gases Come from a Variety of Sources

U.S. Environmental Protection Agency

The U.S. Environmental Protection Agency (EPA) provides comprehensive information on the issue of climate change.

Greenhouse gas emissions have continued to increase in the United States, driven by population growth and increased energy consumption. The largest source of human-generated carbon dioxide emissions in the United States is fossil fuel usage. This includes generating electricity for both home and industrial use, and the use of fossil fuels for transportation. While carbon dioxide exists as a natural component of greenhouse gases, uncovering and using long buried fossil fuels (oil) changes the balance of the natural carbon cycle.

1. *Since 1990, how have greenhouse gas emissions in the U.S. changed?*

Overall, total U.S. emissions have risen by 16.3 percent from 1990 to 2005. This trend is projected to continue at about 1 percent per year assuming current trends in economic growth and fuel consumption continue. The increase is driven principally by population and economic growth, and the rate of change is affected by energy price fluctuations, technological changes, seasonal temperatures, and other factors. On an annual basis, the overall consumption of fossil fuels in the United States generally fluctuates in response to changes in general economic conditions, energy prices, weather, and the

"Emissions," *U.S. Environmental Protection Agency*, December 20, 2007. http://epa.gov/climatechange/fq/emissions.html.

availability of non-fossil alternatives. Future trends will be driven by changes that affect the scale of consumption (e.g., population, number of cars, and size of houses), the efficiency with which energy is used in equipment (e.g., cars, power plants, steel mills, and light bulbs), and consumer behavior (e.g., walking, bicycling, or telecommuting to work instead of driving)....

2. *What are the main greenhouse gases and where do they come from?*

Greenhouse gases include carbon dioxide (CO_2), methane (CH_4), nitrous oxide (N_2O), a number of fluorinated gases, and water vapor (H_2O). Some greenhouse gases occur naturally, such as water vapor and carbon dioxide, while others (such as chlorofluorocarbons) are produced only through human activities. Greenhouse gas inventories account for only those gases whose effects are well-understood (e.g., they include CO_2, CH_4, N_2O, and fluorinated gases, and they include only anthropogenic (human-controlled) sources. Inventories exclude emissions from natural sources (e.g. water vapor)....

The process of generating electricity is the single largest source of emissions in the United States.

---

3. *What are the largest sources of greenhouse gas emissions in the U.S.?*

In the U.S., our energy-related activities account for over three-quarters of our human-generated greenhouse gas emissions, mostly in the form of carbon dioxide emissions from burning fossil fuels. More than half the energy-related emissions come from large sources such as power plants and factories, while about a third comes from transportation. Industrial processes (such as the production of cement, steel, and aluminum), agriculture, other land use, and waste management are also important sources of greenhouse gas emissions in the United States. Forestry is also an important sector—in the U.S., after accounting for tree growth and harvesting, there is a net accumulation of carbon from the atmosphere and into biomass. This net accumulation partially offsets some of the emissions from other sources. . . .

4. *What are greenhouse gas emissions from the power sector?*

The process of generating electricity is the single largest source of emissions in the United States, representing 39 percent of emissions from all sources across the country in 2005. Electricity generation also accounted for the largest share of carbon dioxide emissions from fossil fuel combustion, approximately 41 percent in 2005. Electricity was consumed primarily by users in the residential, commercial, and industrial sectors for lighting, heating, electric motors, appliances, electronics, and air conditioning. . . .

5. *What are greenhouse gas emissions from the transportation sector?*

In the U.S., the transportation sector accounts for approximately 33 percent of total carbon dioxide emissions from fossil fuel combustion, the largest share of any end-use economic sector in 2005. Emissions from this sector increased by 29 percent from 1990 to 2005, representing an average annual increase of 1.8 percent. Over 60 percent of the emissions resulted from gasoline consumption for personal vehicle use. The remaining emissions came from other transportation activities, including the combustion of diesel fuel in heavy-duty vehicles and jet fuel in aircrafts. . . .

Individuals can produce greenhouse gas emissions directly by driving a car or burning oil or gas for home heating.

---

6. *How are individuals contributing to the build-up of greenhouse gases?*

Many daily activities produce greenhouse gas emissions. Individuals can produce greenhouse gas emissions directly by driving a car or burning oil or gas for home heating. Individuals can also produce greenhouse gas emissions indirectly by using electricity generated from fossil fuels. In the United States, emissions per person vary depending on location, habits, and personal choices. For example, the types of fuel used to generate the electricity a person uses can lead to different levels of emissions. A power plant that burns coal emits more greenhouse gases per unit of electricity than a power plant that uses natural gas. How much a person drives, the vehicle's fuel efficiency, and the proportion of driving time spent idling in traffic also affect the level of emissions. In addition, a household's reuse and recycling of materials can affect emissions by reducing the amount of methane-generating waste sent to landfills. EPA's household greenhouse gas emissions calculator provides a good estimate of emissions generated by individuals. . . .

7. How much carbon dioxide do humans contribute through breathing?

The average person, through the natural process of breathing, produces approximately 2.3 pounds of carbon dioxide per day. The actual amount depends strongly on the person's activity level. However, this carbon dioxide is part of a natural closed-loop cycle and does not contribute to the greenhouse gas concentrations in the atmosphere. Natural processes of photosynthesis (in plants) and respiration (in plants and animals) maintain a balance of oxygen and carbon dioxide in the atmosphere. Thus, the carbon dioxide from natural process is not included in greenhouse gas inventories.

In contrast, the burning of fossil fuels upsets this natural equilibrium by adding a surplus of carbon dioxide into the system. The carbon in fossil fuels has been stored underground for millions of years and thus is not part of the current natural carbon cycle. When those fuels are burned, the carbon dioxide generated is over and above the amount circulating from natural sources. Land use changes such as deforestation also upset the natural equilibrium by reducing the amount of carbon dioxide removed from the atmosphere by forests. Thus, both fossil fuel burning and deforestation are accounted for by scientists who develop greenhouse gas inventories to study how greenhouse gases contribute to climate change.

3

Greenhouse Gases Cause Global Warming

Environmental Defense Fund

Environmental Defense Fund is an organization dedicated to finding practical solutions for environmental problems.

There are many myths concerning global warming. Global warming, however, is a scientific fact, caused by an increase of carbon dioxide in the earth's atmosphere from the use of fossil fuels (gas, oil, and coal). Far from creating economic hardship, reducing carbon dioxide will cost families no more than $20 a year. While some critics have stated that increased water vapor causes most global warming, increases in CO_2 (carbon dioxide) levels are responsible for trapping more water vapor in the atmosphere. Global warming will have a devastating impact on the earth's environment, leading to floods, droughts, and heat waves, and will severely effect agriculture. Even now, scientists can project major climate changes, and while fluctuations sometimes create contradictory data, the polar ice caps are melting and sea levels will rise. Global warming is the result of human activities, and will have a devastating effect on future generations unless carbon dioxide emissions are reduced.

MYTH: The science of global warming is too uncertain to act on.

FACT: *There is no debate among scientists about the basic facts of global warming.*

The most respected scientific bodies have stated unequivocally that global warming is occurring, and people are causing it by burning fossil fuels (like coal, oil and natural gas) and cutting down forests. The U.S. National Academy of Sciences, which in 2005 the White House called "the gold standard of objective scientific assessment," issued a joint statement with 10 other National Academies of Science saying "the scientific understanding of climate change is now sufficiently clear to justify nations taking prompt action. It is vital that all nations identify cost-effective steps that they can take now, to contribute to substantial and long-term reduction in net global greenhouse gas emissions." (Joint Statement of Science Academies: Global Response to Climate Change . . . 2005)

The only debate in the science community about global warming is about how much and how fast warming will continue as a result of heat-trapping emissions. Scientists have given a clear warning about global warming, and we have more than enough facts—about causes and fixes—to implement solutions right now.

MYTH: Even if global warming is a problem, addressing it will hurt American industry and workers.

FACT: A well designed trading program will harness American ingenuity to decrease heat-trapping pollution cost-effectively, jumpstarting a new carbon economy.

Claims that fighting global warming will cripple the economy and cost hundreds of thousands of jobs are unfounded. In fact, companies that are already reducing their heat-trapping emissions have discovered that cutting pollution can save money. The cost of a comprehensive national greenhouse gas reduction program will depend on the precise emissions targets, the timing for the reductions and the means of implementation. An independent Massachusetts Institute of Technology [MIT] study found that a modest cap-and-trade system would cost less than $20 per household annually and have no negative impact on employment.

Experience has shown that properly designed emissions trading programs can reduce compliance costs significantly compared with other regulatory approaches. For example, the U.S. acid rain program reduced sulfur dioxide emissions by more than 30 percent from 1990 levels and cost industry a fraction of what the government originally estimated, according to Environmental Protection Agency [EPA]. Furthermore, a mandatory cap on emissions could spur technological innovation that could create jobs and wealth. Letting global warming continue until we are forced to address it on an emergency basis could disrupt and severely damage our economy. It is far wiser and more cost-effective to act now.

MYTH: Water vapor is the most important, abundant greenhouse gas. So if we're going to control a greenhouse gas, why don't we control it instead of carbon dioxide (CO_2)?

FACT: Although water vapor traps more heat than CO_2, because of the relationships among CO_2, water vapor and climate, to fight global warming, nations must focus on controlling CO_2.

Atmospheric levels of CO_2 are determined by how much coal, natural gas and oil we burn and how many trees we cut down, as well as by natural processes like plant growth. Atmospheric levels of water vapor, on the other hand, cannot be directly controlled by people; rather, they are determined by temperatures. The warmer the atmosphere, the more water vapor it can hold. As a result, water vapor is part of an amplifying effect. Greenhouse gases like CO_2 warm the air, which in turn adds to the stock of water vapor, which in turn traps more heat and accelerates warming. Scientists know this because of satellite measurements documenting a rise in water vapor concentrations as the globe has warmed.

The best way to lower temperature and thus reduce water vapor levels is to reduce CO_2 emissions.

MYTH: Global warming and extra CO_2 will actually be beneficial—they reduce cold-related deaths and stimulate crop growth.

FACT: *Any beneficial effects will be far outweighed by damage and disruption.*

Even a warming in just the middle range of scientific projections would have devastating impacts on many sectors of the economy. Rising seas would inundate coastal communities, contaminate water supplies with salt and increase the risk of flooding by storm surge, affecting tens of millions of people globally. Moreover, extreme weather events, including heat waves, droughts and floods, are predicted to increase in frequency and intensity, causing loss of lives and property and throwing agriculture into turmoil.

Even though higher levels of CO_2 can act as a plant fertilizer under some conditions, scientists now think that the "CO_2 fertilization" effect on crops has been overstated; in natural ecosystems, the fertilization effect can diminish after a few years as plants acclimate. Furthermore, increased CO_2 may benefit undesirable, weedy species more than desirable species.

The buildup of CO_2 is the biggest cause of global warming.

Higher levels of CO_2 have already caused ocean acidification, and scientists are warning of potentially devastating effects on marine life and fisheries. Moreover, higher levels of regional ozone (smog), a result of warmer temperatures, could worsen respiratory illnesses. Less developed countries and natural ecosystems may not have the capacity to adapt.

The notion that there will be regional "winners" and "losers" in global warming is based on a world-view from the 1950's. We live in a global community. Never mind the moral implications—when an environmental catastrophe creates millions of refugees half-way around the world, Americans are affected.

MYTH: Global warming is just part of a natural cycle. The Arctic has warmed up in the past.

FACT: The global warming we are experiencing is not natural. People are causing it.

People are causing global warming by burning fossil fuels (like oil, coal and natural gas) and cutting down forests. Scientists have shown that these activities are pumping far more CO_2 into the atmosphere than was ever released in hundreds of thousands of years. This buildup of CO_2 is the biggest cause of global warming. Since 1895, scientists have known that CO_2 and other greenhouse gases trap heat and warm the earth. As the warming has intensified over the past three decades, scientific scrutiny has increased along with it. Scientists have considered and ruled out other, natural explanations such as sunlight, volcanic eruptions and cosmic rays. (IPCC 2001)

Though natural amounts of CO_2 have varied from 180 to 300 parts per million (ppm), today's CO_2 levels are around 380 ppm. That's 25% more than the highest natural levels over the past 650,000 years. Increased CO_2 levels have contributed to periods of higher average temperatures throughout that long record.

The current warming of our climate will bring major hardships and economic dislocations—untold human suffering, especially for our children and grandchildren.

As for previous Arctic warming, it is true that there were stretches of warm periods over the Arctic earlier in the 20th century. The limited records available for that time period indicate that the warmth did not affect as many areas or persist from year to year as much as the current warmth. But that episode, however warm it was, is not relevant to the issue at hand. Why? For one, a brief regional trend does not discount a longer global phenomenon.

We know that the planet has been warming over the past several decades and Arctic ice has been melting persistently. And unlike the earlier periods of Arctic warmth, there is no expectation that the current upward trend in Arctic temperatures will reverse; the rising concentrations of greenhouse gases will prevent that from happening.

MYTH: We can adapt to climate change—civilization has survived droughts and temperature shifts before.

FACT: Although humans as a whole have survived the vagaries of drought, stretches of warmth and cold and more, entire societies have collapsed from dramatic climatic shifts.

The current warming of our climate will bring major hardships and economic dislocations—untold human suffering, especially for our children and grandchildren. We are already seeing significant costs from today's global warming which is caused by greenhouse gas pollution. Climate has changed in the past and human societies have survived, but today six billion people depend on interconnected ecosystems and complex technological infrastructure.

What's more, unless we limit the amount of heat-trapping gases we are putting into the atmosphere, we will face a warming trend unseen since human civilization began 10,000 years ago. (IPCC 2001)

The consequences of continued warming at current rates are likely to be dire. Many densely populated areas, such as low-lying coastal regions, are highly vulnerable to climate shifts. A middle-of-the-range projection is that the homes of 13 to 88 million people around the world would be flooded by the sea each year in the 2080s. Poorer countries and small island nations will have the hardest time adapting. (McLean et al. 2001)

In what appears to be the first forced move resulting from climate change, 100 residents of Tegua island in the Pacific Ocean were evacuated by the government because rising sea levels were flooding their island. Some 2,000 other islanders plan a similar move to escape rising waters. In the United States, the village of Shishmaref in Alaska, which has been inhabited for 400 years, is collapsing from melting permafrost. Relocation plans are in the works.

Scarcity of water and food could lead to major conflicts with broad ripple effects throughout the globe. Even if people find a way to adapt, the wildlife and plants on which we depend may be unable to adapt to rapid climate change. While the world itself will not end, the world as we know it may disappear.

MYTH: Recent cold winters and cool summers don't feel like global warming to me.

FACT: While different pockets of the country have experienced some cold winters here and there, the overall trend is warmer winters.

Measurements show that over the last century the Earth's climate has warmed overall, in all seasons, and in most regions. Climate skeptics mislead the public when they claim that the winter of 2003–2004 was the coldest ever in the northeastern United States. That winter was only the 33rd coldest in the region since records began in 1896. Furthermore, a single year of cold weather in one region of the globe is not an indication of a trend in the global climate, which refers to a long-term average over the entire planet.

Between 1961 and 1997, the world's glaciers lost 890 cubic miles of ice.

MYTH: Global warming can't be happening because some glaciers and ice sheets are growing, not shrinking.

FACT: In most parts of the world, the retreat of glaciers has been dramatic. The best available scientific data indicate that Greenland's massive ice sheet is shrinking.

Between 1961 and 1997, the world's glaciers lost 890 cubic miles of ice. The consensus among scientists is that rising air temperatures are the most important factor behind the retreat of glaciers on a global scale over long time periods. Some glaciers in western Norway, Iceland and New Zealand have been expanding during the past few decades. That expansion is a result of regional increases in storm frequency and snowfall rather than colder temperatures—not at all incompatible with a global warming trend.

In Greenland, a NASA [National Aeronautics and Space Administration] satellite that can measure the ice mass over the whole continent has found that although there is variation from month to month, over the longer term, the ice is disappearing. In fact, there are worrisome signs that melting is accelerating: glaciers are moving into the ocean twice as fast as a decade ago, and, over time, more and more glaciers have started to accelerate. What is most alarming is the prediction, based on model calculations and historical evidence, that an approximately 5.4 degree Fahrenheit increase in local Greenland temperatures will lead to irreversible meltdown and a sea-level rise of over 20 feet. Since the Arctic is warming 2–3 times faster than the global average, this tipping point is not far away.

The only study that has shown increasing ice mass in Greenland only looked at the interior of the ice sheet, not at the edges where melting occurs. This is actually in line with climate model predictions that global warming would lead to a short-term accumulation of ice in the cold interior due to heavier snowfall. (Similarly, scientists have predicted that Antarctica overall will gain ice in the near future due to heavier snowfall.) The scientists who published the study were careful to point out that their results should not be used to conclude that Greenland's ice mass as a whole is growing. In addition, their data suggested that the accumulation of snow in the middle of the continent is likely to decrease over time as global warming continues.

MYTH: Accurate weather predictions a few days in advance are hard to come by. Why on earth should we have confidence in climate projections decades from now?

FACT: Climate prediction is fundamentally different from weather prediction, just as climate is different from weather.

It is often more difficult to make an accurate weather forecast than a climate prediction. The accuracy of weather forecasting is critically dependent upon being able to exactly and comprehensively characterize the present state of the global atmosphere. Climate prediction relies on other, longer ranging factors. For instance, we might not know if it will be below freezing on a specific December day in New England, but we know from our understanding of the region's climate that the temperatures during the month will generally be low. Similarly, climate tells us that Seattle and London tend to be rainy, Florida and southern California are usually warm, and the Southwest is often dry and hot.

Today's climate models can now reproduce the observed global average climates over the past century and beyond. Such findings have reinforced scientist's confidence in the capacity of models to produce reliable projections of future climate. Current climate assessments typically consider the results from a range of models and scenarios for future heat-trapping emissions in order to identify the most likely range for future climatic change.

MYTH: As the ozone hole shrinks, global warming will no longer be a problem.

FACT: Global warming and the ozone hole are two different problems.

The ozone hole is a thinning of the stratosphere's ozone layer, which is roughly 9 to 31 miles above the earth's surface. The depletion of the ozone is due to man-made chemicals like chlorofluorocarbons (CFCs). A thinner ozone layer lets more harmful ultraviolet (UV) radiation to reach the earth's surface.

Global warming, on the other hand, is the increase in the earth's average temperature due to the buildup of CO_2 and other greenhouse gases in the atmosphere from human activities.

4

Greenhouse Gases Do Not Cause Global Warming

David Bellamy

David Bellamy is an English botanist who has written frequently on global warming.

While many within and without the scientific community have tried to convince the public that carbon dioxide causes global warming, they have been unable to prove the link. In truth, climate change has been a fact throughout history, with temperatures rising and falling in no relation to carbon dioxide levels. Critics of carbon emissions also ignore the influence of solar cycles, cosmic rays, and other factors that increase global warming. They also distort facts, spending billions of dollars on propaganda. Most of the fluctuations that scientists worry about now have occurred at earlier points in history—before the presence of human-made carbon dioxide.

A m I worried about man-made global warming? The answer is "no" and "yes".

No, because the Hadley Centre for Climate Prediction has come up against an "inconvenient truth". Its research shows that since 1998 the average temperature of the planet has not risen, even though the concentration of carbon dioxide in the atmosphere has continued to increase.

Yes, because the self-proclaimed consensus among scientists has detached itself from the questioning rigours of hard

David Bellamy, "Today's Forecast: Yet Another Blast of Hot Air," *The Times*, October 22, 2007. p. 5. Copyright © 2008 Times Newspapers Ltd. Reproduced by permission. www.timesonline.co.uk/tol/comment/columnists/guest_contributors/article2709551.ecc.

science and become a political cause. Those of us who dare to question the dogma of the global-warming doomsters who claim that C not only stands for carbon but also for climate catastrophe are vilified as heretics or worse as deniers.

The truth is that there are no facts that link the concentration of atmospheric carbon dioxide with imminent catastrophic global warming.

I am happy to be branded a heretic because throughout history heretics have stood up against dogma based on the bigotry of vested interests. But I don't like being smeared as a denier because deniers don't believe in facts. The truth is that there are no facts that link the concentration of atmospheric carbon dioxide with imminent catastrophic global warming. Instead of facts, the advocates of man-made climate change trade in future scenarios based on complex and often unreliable computer models.

Name-calling may be acceptable in politics but it should have no place in science; indeed, what is happening smacks of McCarthyism [the period in the early 1950s when Senator Joseph McCarthy and others accused many innocent American citizens of being communists], witch-hunts and all. Scientific understanding, however, is advanced by robust, reasoned argument base on well-researched data. So I turn to simple sets of data that are already in the public domain.

History and Climate Change

The last peak global temperatures were in 1998 and 1934 and the troughs of low temperature were around 1910 and 1970. The second dip caused pop science and the media to cry wolf about an impending, devastating Ice Age. Our end was nigh!

Then, when temperatures took an upward swing in the 1980s, the scaremongers changed their tune. Global warming was the new imminent catastrophe.

But the computer model—called "hockey stick"—that predicted the catastrophe of a frying planet proved to be so bent that it "disappeared" from the Intergovernmental Panel on Climate Change's armoury of argument in 2007. It was bent because the historical data it used to predict the future dated from only the 1850s, when the world was emerging from the Little Ice Age. Little wonder that temperatures showed an upward trend.

In the Sixties I used to discuss climate change with my undergraduates at Durham University. I would point to the plethora of published scientific evidence that showed the cyclical nature of change—and how, for instance, the latest of a string of ice ages had affected the climate, sea levels and tree lines around the world. Thank goodness the latest crop of glaciers and ice sheets began to wane in earnest about 12,000 years ago; this gave Britain a window of opportunity to lead the industrial revolution.

The Romans grew grapes in York and during the worldwide medieval warm period—when civilizations blossomed across the world—Nordic settlers farmed lowland Greenland (hence its name) and then got wiped out by the Little Ice Age that lasted roughly from the 16th century until about 1850.

Not only have there been long periods of little change in temperature, but also the year-to-year oscillations are totally unrelated to CO_2 change.

There is no escaping the fact that the concentration of carbon dioxide in the atmosphere has been rising for 150 years—and very uniformly since the 1950s. Yet the temperature has not increased in step with CO_2. Not only have there been long periods of little change in temperature, but also the year-to-year oscillations are totally unrelated to CO_2 change.

What is more, the trend lines of glacial shortening and rise in sea level have shown no marked change since the big increase in the use of fossil fuels since 1950.

Inconvenient Truths

How can this be explained unless there are other factors at work overriding the greenhouse effect of CO_2? There are, of course, many to be found in the peer-reviewed literature: solar cycles, cosmic rays, cloud control and those little rascals, such as El Niño and La Niña, all of which are played down or even ignored by the global-warming brigade.

Despite the $50 billion spent on greenwashing propaganda, the skeptics and their inconvenient questions are beginning to make their presence felt.

Let's turn to Al Gore's doom-laden Oscar-winning documentary *An Inconvenient Truth*. First, what is the point of scaring the families of the world with tales that polar bears are heading for extinction? Last year Mitchell Taylor, of the US National Biological Service, stated that "of the 13 populations of polar bears in Canada, 11 are stable or increasing in number. They are not going extinct, or even appear to be affected at present."

Why create alarm about a potential increase in the spread of malaria thanks to rising temperatures when this mosquito-borne disease was a major killer of people in Britain and northern Russia throughout the Little Ice Age?

Despite the $50 billion spent on greenwashing propaganda, the sceptics and their inconvenient questions are beginning to make their presence felt.

A recent survey of Klaus-Martin Schulte, of Kings College Hospital, of all papers on the subject of climate change that were published between 2004 and February of 2007 found that only 7 per cent explicitly endorsed a "so-called consensus" position that man-made carbon dioxide is causing catastrophic global warming. What is more, James Lovelock, the author and green guru, has changed his mind: he recently stated that neither Earth nor the human race is doomed.

Historical Fluctuations

Yes, melting sea ice around Greenland has recently opened up the fabled North West passage. And, yes, the years 2006 and 2007 have seen massive flooding in Europe. However, a quick dip into the records of the Royal Society—which ranked alongside Dr Lovelock as arch doomsters, before his change of mind—shows that dramatic fluctuations happened long before the infernal combustion engine began spewing out carbon dioxide.

The year 1816 went down in history as the "year without a summer", thanks to the eruption of Mount Tambora in Indonesia that veiled much of the world with dust, screening out the Sun. Yet in 1817, while still in the grip of the Little Ice Age, the Royal Society was so worried that 2,000 square leagues of sea ice around Greenland had disappeared within two years, and massive flooding was taking place in Germany, that its president wrote to the Admiralty advising of the necessity of an expedition to find out what was the source of this new heat.

Perhaps, when similar things are happening 190 years later, the Royal Society should accept that anthropogenic carbon dioxide is unlikely to be the main—or only—driver of "global warming".

5

Global Warming Is Caused by a Climate Cycle, Not Greenhouse Gases

Dennis T. Avery

Dennis T. Avery is a senior fellow of the Hudson Institute and the author of Unstoppable Global Warming *with Fred Singer.*

More and more, Americans have been told that they should use less fossil fuel to curtail the greenhouse gases that cause global warming. That the earth is growing warmer is undoubtedly true: but how much of that change is really connected to greenhouse gases? In truth, climate fluctuations have happened in the past, even before the availability of human-made fossil fuels. Looking at ice cores that can be dated back 900,000 years, a pattern develops: a 1500-year cycle increases temperatures two degrees above average before dropping the temperature two degrees below average. This change is tied to solar activity, not carbon gases. Despite popular wisdom, the increase in the earth's temperature is triggering the increased presence of carbon dioxide in the atmosphere, not vice versa.

Should America give up fossil fuels, cars, and air conditioning?

Should we ration electricity from noisy, erratic windmills, while ignoring trillions of barrels of low-grade petroleum in bitumen deposits that could cost-effectively power our society for another 200 years?

Should we vote for a Greenhouse Theory that can't explain Earth's recent climate changes?

Or should we examine the new but already-convincing evidence that the Modern Warming is part of the Earth's unstoppable, moderate, solar-driven 1500-year climate cycle?

There's no question the Earth has warmed over the last 150 years. We're no longer in the Little Ice Age—thank goodness. Glaciers are retreating and winters are a bit milder.

The real question is why?

What Causes Global Warming?

Persistent voices say Earth is warming dangerously, due to human-emitted CO_2. If that is the case, then why did virtually all of the Earth's warming occur before 1940—before the world had many factories or autos? CO_2 emissions have soared since 1940, but today's temperatures aren't significantly higher.

The Greenhouse Theory says trapped CO_2 will heat the atmosphere above us. That heat then will radiate down to warm the Earth. But that hasn't happened. The atmosphere is warming much more slowly than the Earth's surface—at 1 degree C per 300 years, according to the satellites.

We know the Earth has a varied climate history.

The polar regions are supposed to overheat first. But the polar regions are *cooling.* Arctic temperatures were higher in the 1930s than they are now. Twenty-one Antarctic surface stations show a decline of 0.08 degrees C since 1979.

We know the Earth has a varied climate history. Medieval monks wrote that the 12th century was very warm; and humans prospered. During the Little Ice Age, in 1816, the Connecticut summer was 2.5 degrees C colder than the mean of 1780–1968. London held its last ice festival on the Thames River in 1814 because the river quit freezing.

Ice cores take us back through 900,000 years of Ice Ages—sudden coolings—and pleasant interglacials like our own. Through it all runs a moderate 1500-year cycle that raises temperatures in New York and Northern Europe about 2 degrees C above the long-term average during its warming phases—just like the Roman and Medieval warmings. Then it lowers temperatures about 2 degrees below the long-term average during the mini-Ice Ages. The temperatures at the equator change hardly at all, although the rainfall patterns do.

The 1500-Year Cycle

The 1500-year cycle was too long and too moderate to be sung in the Norse sagas, though the Vikings' Greenland colonies thrived during the Medieval Warming and froze to death in the Little Ice Age.

The cycle is tied to a tiny variation in solar activity that we can now measure from space with satellite instruments, and measure in history through carbon and beryllium isotopes in the ice cores.

Humanity could stop burning fossil fuels tomorrow, but it wouldn't stop the climate cycle that has warmed the Earth slowly and erratically for the last 150 years.

We find the cycle globally—in the Greenland ice sheet, in Antarctic glaciers, in seabed sediments from the Atlantic and the Indian Oceans, in ancient tree rings from around the Northern Hemisphere, in the relocations of primitive Andean villages, and in cave stalagmites from Ireland, Arabia and South Africa.

The North American Pollen Data Base shows our vegetation completely reorganized by climate change nine times in the past 14,000 years. That's once every 1650 years.

The Antarctic ice cores say CO_2 and temperatures have tracked closely together over the past 400,000 years. But CO_2

changes have lagged behind the temperature changes by 200–800 years. More CO_2 *hasn't* produced higher temperatures; higher temperatures have produced more CO_2.

Humanity could stop burning fossil fuels tomorrow, but it wouldn't stop the climate cycle that has warmed the Earth slowly and erratically for the last 150 years. When the warming ends in another few centuries the cycle will give us colder temperatures. That's when we'll really need to worry about heat.

6

There Is No Scientific Consensus on Global Warming

Richard S. Lindzen

Richard S. Lindzen is the Alfred P. Sloan Professor of Atmospheric Science at MIT.

Champions of global warming like Al Gore would like to convince the public that there is a scientific consensus on the connection between climate change and carbon dioxide. Furthermore, they claim that the debate on global warming is over, conveniently ignoring any evidence offered by more skeptical scientists. In fact, the so-called consensus on global warming ignores a great deal of evidence that counters its argument. Even while most scientists agree that global warming is taking place and that there has been an atmospheric increase in carbon dioxide, no one has proven a cause and effect connection between the two. Instead, global warming "champions" have inferred the connection without having a solid understanding of historical variations that might effect climate fluctuations. Finally, the claim of consensus is simply misleading, allowing non-scientists—politicians and environmentalists—easy answers to complex questions.

According to Al Gore's new film *An Inconvenient Truth*, we're in for "a planetary emergency": melting ice sheets, huge increases in sea levels, more and stronger hurricanes, and invasions of tropical disease, among other cataclysms—unless we change the way we live now.

Bill Clinton has become the latest evangelist for Mr. Gore's gospel, proclaiming that current weather events show that he and Mr. Gore were right about global warming, and we are all suffering the consequences of President [George W.] Bush's obtuseness on the matter. And why not? Mr. Gore assures us that "the debate in the scientific community is over."

Is there really a scientific community that is debating all of these issues and then somehow agreeing in unison?

That statement, which Mr. Gore made in an interview with George Stephanopoulos on ABC, ought to have been followed by an asterisk. What exactly is this debate that Mr. Gore is referring to? Is there really a scientific community that is debating all these issues and then somehow agreeing in unison? Far from such a thing being over, it has never been clear to me what this "debate" actually is in the first place.

A Scientific Consensus?

The media rarely help, of course. When *Newsweek* featured global warming in a 1988 issue, it was claimed that all scientists agreed. Periodically thereafter it was revealed that although there had been lingering doubts beforehand, *now* all scientists did indeed agree. Even Mr. Gore qualified his statement on ABC only a few minutes after he made it, clarifying things in an important way. When Mr. Stephanopoulos confronted Mr. Gore with the fact that the best estimates of rising sea levels are far less dire than he suggests in his movie, Mr. Gore defended his claims by noting that scientists "don't have any models that give them a high level of confidence" one way or the other and went on to claim—*in his defense*—that scientists "don't know. . . . They just don't know."

So, presumably, those scientists do not belong to the "consensus." Yet their research is forced, whether the evidence supports it or not, into Mr. Gore's preferred global-warming template—namely, shrill alarmism. To believe it requires that one ignore the truly inconvenient facts. To take the issue of rising sea levels, these include: that the Arctic was as warm or warmer in 1940; that icebergs have been known since time immemorial; that the evidence so far suggests that the Greenland ice sheet is actually growing on average. A likely result of all this is increased pressure pushing ice off the coastal perimeter of that country, which is depicted so ominously in Mr. Gore's movie. In the absence of factual context, these images are perhaps dire or alarming.

They are less so otherwise. Alpine glaciers have been retreating since the early 19th century, and were advancing for several centuries before that. Since about 1970, many of the glaciers have stopped retreating and some are now advancing again. And, frankly, we don't know why.

Even among those arguing, there is general agreement that we can't attribute any particular hurricane to global warming.

Global Warming Oversights

The other elements of the global-warming scare scenario are predicated on similar oversights. Malaria, claimed as a byproduct of warming, was once common in Michigan and Siberia and remains common in Siberia—mosquitoes don't require tropical warmth. Hurricanes, too, vary on multidecadal time scales; sea-surface temperature is likely to be an important factor. This temperature, itself, varies on multidecadal time scales. However, questions concerning the origin of the relevant sea-surface temperatures and the nature of trends in hurricane intensity are being hotly argued within the profession.

Even among those arguing, there is general agreement that we can't attribute any particular hurricane to global warming.

To be sure, there is one exception, Greg Holland of the National Center for Atmospheric Research in Boulder, Colo., who argues that it must be global warming because he can't think of anything else. While arguments like these, based on lassitude, are becoming rather common in climate assessments, such claims, given the primitive state of weather and climate science, are hardly compelling.

A general characteristic of Mr. Gore's approach is to assiduously ignore the fact that the earth and its climate are dynamic; they are always changing even without any external forcing. To treat all change as something to fear is bad enough; to do so in order to exploit that fear is much worse. Regardless, these items are clearly not issues over which debate is ended—at least not in terms of the actual science.

Connecting Carbon Dioxide to Global Warming

A clearer claim as to what debate has ended is provided by the environmental journalist Gregg Easterbrook. He concludes that the scientific community now agrees that significant warming is occurring, and that there is clear evidence of human influences on the climate system. This is still a most peculiar claim. At some level, it has never been widely contested. Most of the climate community has agreed since 1988 that global mean temperatures have increased on the order of one degree Fahrenheit over the past century, having risen significantly from about 1919 to 1940, decreased between 1940 and the early '70s, increased again until the '90s, and remaining essentially flat since 1998.

There is also little disagreement that levels of carbon dioxide in the atmosphere have risen from about 280 parts per million by volume in the 19th century to about 387 ppmv today. Finally, there has been no question whatever that carbon dioxide is an infrared absorber (i.e., a greenhouse gas—albeit a minor one), and its increase should theoretically contribute to warming. Indeed, if all else were kept equal, the increase in carbon dioxide should have led to somewhat more warming than has been observed, assuming that the small observed increase was in fact due to increasing carbon dioxide rather than a natural fluctuation in the climate system. Although no cause for alarm rests on this issue, there has been an intense effort to claim that the theoretically expected contribution from additional carbon dioxide has actually been detected.

Given that we do not understand the natural internal variability of climate change, this task is currently impossible. Nevertheless there has been a persistent effort to suggest otherwise, and with surprising impact. Thus, although the conflicted state of the affair was accurately presented in the 1996 text of the Intergovernmental Panel on Climate Change, the infamous "summary for policy makers" reported ambiguously that "The balance of evidence suggests a discernible human influence on global climate." This sufficed as the smoking gun for Kyoto.

The next IPCC report again described the problems surrounding what has become known as the attribution issue: that is, to explain what mechanisms are responsible for observed changes in climate. Some deployed the lassitude argument—e.g., we can't think of an alternative—to support human attribution. But the "summary for policy makers" claimed in a manner largely unrelated to the actual text of the report that "In the light of new evidence and taking into account the remaining uncertainties, most of the observed warming over the last 50 years is likely to have been due to the increase in greenhouse gas concentrations."

Insufficient Evidence

In a similar vein, the National Academy of Sciences issued a brief (15-page) report responding to questions from the White House. It again enumerated the difficulties with attribution, but again the report was preceded by a front end that ambiguously claimed that "The changes observed over the last several decades are likely mostly due to human activities, but we cannot rule out that some significant part of these changes is also a reflection of natural variability." This was sufficient for CNN's Michelle Mitchell to presciently declare that the report represented a "unanimous decision that global warming is real, is getting worse and is due to man. There is no wiggle room." Well, no.

More recently, a study in the journal *Science* by the social scientist Nancy Oreskes claimed that a search of the ISI Web of Knowledge Database for the years 1993 to 2003 under the key words "global climate change" produced 928 articles, all of whose abstracts supported what she referred to as the consensus view. A British social scientist, Benny Peiser, checked her procedure and found that only 913 of the 928 articles had abstracts at all, and that only 13 of the remaining 913 explicitly endorsed the so-called consensus view. Several actually opposed it.

There is a clear attempt to establish truth not by scientific methods but by perpetual repetition.

Even more recently, the Climate Change Science Program, the Bush administration's coordinating agency for global-warming research, declared it had found "clear evidence of human influences on the climate system." This, for Mr. Easterbrook, meant: "Case closed." What exactly was this evidence? The models imply that greenhouse warming should impact atmospheric temperatures more than surface temperatures, and yet satellite data showed no warming in the atmosphere since 1979. The report showed that selective corrections to the atmospheric data could lead to some warming, thus reducing the conflict between observations and models descriptions of what greenhouse warming should look like. That, to me, means the case is still very much open.

False Claims of Consensus

So what, then, is one to make of this alleged debate? I would suggest at least three points.

First, nonscientists generally do not want to bother with understanding the science. Claims of consensus relieve policy types, environmental advocates and politicians of any need to do so. Such claims also serve to intimidate the public and even scientists—especially those outside the area of climate dynamics. Secondly, given that the question of human attribution largely cannot be resolved, its use in promoting visions of disaster constitutes nothing so much as a bait-and-switch scam. That is an inauspicious beginning to what Mr. Gore claims is not a political issue but a "moral" crusade.

Lastly, there is a clear attempt to establish truth not by scientific methods but by perpetual repetition. An earlier attempt at this was accompanied by tragedy. Perhaps Marx was right. This time around we may have farce—if we're lucky.

7

There Is a Scientific Consensus on Global Warming

Naomi Oreskes

Naomi Oreskes is an associate professor of history and director of the Science Studies program at the University of California, San Diego.

Despite much disinformation, there is a scientific consensus on global warming. Multiple scientific organizations agree that human activities, mainly the creation of greenhouse gases, are causing the earth's atmosphere to grow warmer. A review of scientific abstracts likewise confirms scientific agreement on global warming. Why, then, does there appear to be disagreement? Because skeptical non-scientists have been able to air their views through the popular media. Unfortunately, these skeptical points of view are distracting the public from the need to respond to the global warming crisis.

Many people have the impression that there is significant scientific disagreement about global climate change. It's time to lay that misapprehension to rest. There is a scientific consensus on the fact that Earth's climate is heating up and human activities are part of the reason. We need to stop repeating nonsense about the uncertainty of global warming and start talking seriously about the right approach to address it.

Naomi Oreskes, "Undeniable Global Warming," *Washington Post*, December 26, 2004, p. 4. © The Washington Post Company. Reproduced by permission of the author. www.washingtonpost.com/wp-dyn/articles/A26065-2004Dec25.html.

The scientific consensus is clearly expressed in the reports of the Intergovernmental Panel on Climate Change (IPCC). Created in 1988 by the World Meteorological Organization and the United Nations Environmental Program, the IPCC is charged with evaluating the state of climate science as a basis for informed policy action. In its most recent assessment, the IPCC states unequivocally that the consensus of scientific opinion is that Earth's climate is being affected by human activities: "Human activities . . . are modifying the concentration of atmospheric constituents . . . that absorb or scatter radiant energy. . . . Most of the observed warming over the last 50 years is likely to have been due to the increase in greenhouse gas concentrations."

The IPCC is not alone in its conclusions. In recent years all major scientific bodies in the United States whose members' expertise bears directly on the matter have issued similar statements. A National Academy of Sciences report begins unequivocally: "Greenhouse gases are accumulating in Earth's atmosphere as a result of human activities, causing surface air temperatures and subsurface ocean temperatures to rise." The report explicitly asks whether the IPCC assessment is a fair summary of professional scientific thinking, and it answers yes. Others agree. The American Meteorological Society, the American Geophysical Union and the American Association for the Advancement of Science have all issued statements concluding that the evidence for human modification of climate is compelling.

Scientific Agreement on Global Warming

Despite recent allegations to the contrary, these statements from the leadership of scientific societies and the IPCC accurately reflect the state of the art in climate science research. The Institute for Scientific Information keeps a database on published scientific articles, which my research assistants and I used to answer that question with respect to global climate change. We read 928 abstracts published in scientific journals between 1993 and 2003 and listed in the database with the keywords "global climate change." Seventy-five percent of the papers either explicitly or implicitly accepted the consensus view. The remaining 25 percent dealt with other facets of the subject, taking no position on whether current climate change is caused by human activity. None of the papers disagreed with the consensus position. There have been arguments to the contrary, but they are not to be found in scientific literature, which is where scientific debates are properly adjudicated. There, the message is clear and unambiguous.

The chatter of skeptics is distracting us from the real issue: how best to respond to the threats that global warming presents.

To be sure, a handful of scientists have raised questions about the details of climate models, about the accuracy of methods for evaluating past global temperatures and about the wisdom of even attempting to predict the future. But this is quibbling about the details. The basic picture is clear, and some changes are already occurring. A new report by the Arctic Climate Impact Assessment—a consortium of eight countries, including Russia and the United States—now confirms that major changes are taking place in the Arctic, affecting both human and non-human communities, as predicted by climate models. This information was conveyed to the U.S. Senate last month not by a radical environmentalist, as was recently alleged on the Web, but by Robert Corell, a senior fellow of the American Meteorological Society and former assistant director for geosciences at the National Science Foundation.

So why does it seem as if there is major scientific disagreement? Because a few noisy skeptics—most of whom are not even scientists—have generated a lot of chatter in the mass media. At the National Press Club recently, Massachusetts Institute of Technology professor Richard Lindzen dismissed the consensus as "religious belief." To be sure, no scientific conclusion can ever be proven, absolutely, but it is no more a "belief" to say that Earth is heating up than it is to say that continents move, that germs cause disease, that DNA carries hereditary information or that quarks are the basic building blocks of subatomic matter. You can always find someone, somewhere, to disagree, but these conclusions represent our best available science, and therefore our best basis for reasoned action.

The chatter of skeptics is distracting us from the real issue: how best to respond to the threats that global warming presents.

8

Global Stewardship Requires Controlling Greenhouse Gases

The editors of America

America *is a national Catholic weekly.*

The Bible presented two dictates to Adam and Eve, first telling them to be fruitful and conquer the earth, and next, softening the first command by asking them to cultivate and take care of the Garden of Eden. The latter presents the idea of stewardship. Today, however, fewer people speak of human accomplishments and stewardship; instead, they highlight the dark side of technology. This has been especially evident in regard to the environment, where there is a growing consensus focusing on the connection between greenhouse gases and global warming. By raising the temperature of the ocean and earth, global warming has the potential to cause great harm to both humans and animals. Understanding the scientific consensus on global warming, people should begin taking steps to protect the earth by curbing greenhouse emissions.

In their accounts of the divine creation, the mysterious opening pages of the Bible twice indicate that the work men and women do is neither a penalty nor a curse but an essential human experience toward which these creatures were naturally oriented even before the Fall. In the first chapter of Genesis, God is described as blessing Adam and Eve and commissioning them: "Be fruitful, multiply, fill the earth and conquer it." In the next chapter, this vocation is reaffirmed but nuanced: "Yahweh God took the man and settled him in the garden of Eden to cultivate and take care of it." The call to master the earth is not reversed, but it is qualified. The human family should draw upon the globe's resources but in the spirit of a steward who conserves as well as consumes.

In his 1953 Christmas message, Pope Pius XII cited this biblical directive and added a commentary: "What a long and hard road from then to the present day when men can at last say that they have in some measure fulfilled the divine command. . . ."

Nowadays, however, there is less talk about the achievements of homo faber—man the maker—than about the dark side of mechanized industrial technology and particularly about the damage it has done to the natural environment. For several decades, scientists who study the climate have been warning of this danger and thoughtful people, ranging from journalists to religious leaders, have listened. In his message for the World Day of Peace on Jan. 1, 1990, for instance, Pope John Paul II began by saying that there is today a growing awareness that world peace is threatened not only by the arms race, regional conflicts and injustice but also by an ecological crisis, which has been created by "a lack of due respect for nature."

Together these gas emissions have raised air and ocean temperatures worldwide and amount to catastrophes in the making.

Global Warming Consensus

The most frightening manifestation of this crisis is the phenomenon called global warming. Earlier this month [Feb., 2007], the latest news about this peril made the front page of papers like *The New York Times* and *The Washington Post* and should have resounded everywhere, like a firebell in the night. In Paris, the Intergovernmental Panel on Climate Change issued a summary of the most recent studies of the effects on the global climate of what are called greenhouse gas emissions. These gases are chiefly carbon dioxide, methane and nitrous oxide released into the atmosphere from the smokestacks of factories, the tailpipes of automobiles and a countless number of smaller machines as well as from burning forests.

Together these gas emissions have raised air and ocean temperatures worldwide and amount to catastrophes in the making. They are already melting the arctic sea ice and adjoining ice sheets, leaving puzzled polar bears stranded on ice floes. Rises in sea levels may sweep away the homes of people living on seacoast plains, scientists warn, and heat waves are expected to disrupt agriculture.

A tiny band of dissenters thinks the specter of global warming is a hoax, and some commentators think its dangers have been exaggerated; but the proponents received strong support from the Intergovernmental Panel on Global Climate Change. The panel, founded in 1988 and sponsored by the United Nations, has reviewed the research of hundreds of investigators. Through their representatives, some 113 nations, including the United States, have ratified the panel's findings.

These conclusions are principally two. First, global warming is not a conjecture but a fact—"unequivocal," the panel says. Panel members are 90 percent certain that human activity embodied in technology has built up the greenhouse gases that are the source of this warming. Second, those looming disastrous consequences can be eliminated or diminished by drastically reducing greenhouse gas emissions at once.

Global Warming and Stewardship

In his 1990 message, Pope John Paul II called the ecological crisis a common responsibility. But what can individuals do? Two things. First, they can support the far-sighted initiatives of public officials. California's Gov. Arnold Schwarzenegger, for example, was able to push through the legislature laws capping greenhouse gas emissions, because a sufficient number of voters backed him. Such standards need to be replicated across the states and by the federal government. Second, citizens can act on their own. In the movie and book *An Inconvenient Truth*, former Vice President Al Gore recommends more than a dozen steps—from running the dishwasher only with a full load to using car pools. Shifts in consumer preferences, as we saw in the energy crisis of the 1970's, can help make a difference.

Here is some good advice with a biblical flavor: God designed the earth, says the prophet, not to be a wasteland but to be lived in.

9

Greenhouse Gas Reductions Should Calculate Economic Impact

William F. Buckley, Jr.

William F. Buckley, Jr. (1925–2008) was the founding editor of the National Review.

The issue of global warming has taken on the aura of a religious crusade, with environmentalists condemning anyone who disagrees with the consensus. The problem is that while it may be easy to agree that human activity is impacting the earth's atmosphere, no one can measure the potential damage accurately. Other problems persist. If the United States is the chief global warming offender, then it could slow global warming by reducing the use of fossil fuels. Still, this may have little impact if other countries like China and India continue to increase their consumption of fossil fuels. Also, few have considered the economic impact of following the Kyoto Accord (an international environmental agreement). The agreement, if signed by the United States, could potentially cost $100 to $400 billion per year.

The heavy condemnatory breathing on the subject of global warming outdoes anything since high moments of the Inquisition. A respectable columnist (Thomas Friedman of the *New York Times*) opened his essay last week by writing, "Sometimes you read something about this administration that's just so shameful it takes your breath away."

What asphyxiated this critic was the discovery that a White House official had edited "government climate reports to play up uncertainty of a human role in global warming." The correspondent advises that the culprit had been an oil-industry lobbyist before joining the administration, and on leaving it he took a job with ExxonMobil.

For those with addled reflexes, here is the story compressed: (1) Anyone who speaks discriminatingly about global warming is conspiring to belittle the threat. Such people end up (2) working for ExxonMobil, a perpetrator of the great threat the malefactor sought to distract us from.

Critics are correct in insisting that human enterprises have an effect on climate.

In the current mood, I should enter the datum that my father was in the oil business. But having done that, I think it fair to ask: Are we invited to assume that anyone who works in a business that generates greenhouse gases (a) is complicit in the global-warming problem, and (b) should resign and seek work elsewhere?

The Economic Impact of Conservation

Critics are correct in insisting that human enterprises have an effect on climate. What they cannot at this point do is specify exactly how great the damage is, nor how much relief would be effected by specific acts of natural propitiation.

The whole business is eerily religious in feel. Back in the 15th century, the question was: Do you believe in Christ? It was required in Spain by the Inquisition that the answer should be affirmative, leaving to one side subsidiary specifications.

It is required today to believe that carbon-dioxide emissions threaten the ecological balance. The assumption then is that inasmuch as a large proportion of the damage is man-made, man-made solutions are necessary. But it is easy to see, right away, that there is a problem in devising appropriate solutions, and in allocating responsibility for them.

To speak in very general terms, the U.S. is easily the principal offender, given our size and the intensity of our use of fossil-fuel energy. But even accepting the high per capita rate of consumption in the United States, we face the terrible inadequacy of ameliorative resources. If the USA were (we are dealing in hypotheses) to eliminate the use of oil or gas for power, would that forfeiture be decisive?

Well, no. It would produce about 23 percent global relief, and at a devastating cost to our economy.

The International Dimension

As a practical matter, what have modern states undertaken with a view to diminishing greenhouse gases? The answer is: Not very much. What is being done gives off a kind of satisfaction, of the kind felt back then when prayers were recited as apostates were led to the stake. If you levied a 100 percent surtax on gasoline in the United States, you would certainly reduce the use of it, but the arbiter is there to say: What is a complementary sacrifice we can then expect from India and China? China will soon overtake the U.S. in the production of greenhouse gases.

At Kyoto, an effort was made 10 years ago to allocate proportional reductions nation by nation. The United States almost uniquely declined to subscribe to the protocols. Canada, Japan, and the countries of Western Europe subscribed, but some have already fallen short of their goals, and all of them are skeptical about the prospect of future scheduled reductions. It is estimated that if the U.S. had subscribed to Kyoto, it would have cost us $100 billion to $400 billion per year.

There is, now and then, offsetting good news. The next report from the Intergovernmental Panel on Climate Change (IPCC), we have learned, will be less pessimistic than earlier reports. It will predict, e.g., a sea-level increase of up to 23 inches by the end of the century, substantially better than earlier IPCC predictions of 29 inches—and light-years away from the 20 feet predicted by Al Gore.

Meanwhile, the Danish statistician Bjorn Lomborg said something outside the hearing of the outraged columnist. He noted solemnly that any increase in heat-related deaths should be balanced against the corresponding decrease in cold-related deaths. . . . We need hope, and self-confidence.

10

A Global Effort Is Needed to Reduce Greenhouse Gases

Bill McKibben

Bill McKibben is an author, educator, and environmentalist.

It is easy to despair when considering the dire consequences of global warming. Despair, however, only distracts from the need for action. First, we should understand that action must be taken soon to curtail global warming. Next, in order to reduce our reliance on fossil fuels, we need to replace our energy systems. Still, the obstacles are daunting. Americans need to realize that other nations (India and China) have also begun to rely heavily on fossil fuels, compounding the problem, and that oil companies have little incentive to consider radical change when profits are at an all-time high. People are beginning to organize, however, expressing a commitment to change.

For years too many people ignored global warming—it wasn't "proven," it was a "hypothesis," it was "doomsaying," It was too small, too distant, to worry about.

But that's not the problem anymore, not since Katrina. Now it's just the opposite—the problem's too big. We all read headlines every few days about the inexorable melt of Arctic ice, about record drought, about big new storms, I'm writing these words the day after the second Category 5 hurricane of the season has made an Atlantic landfall—the first time that's ever happened. And you're going to fix it by changing your lightbulb?

Bill McKibben, "Let's Act Together on Global Warming," *Tikkun*, November-December, 2007, p. 5. Copyright © 2007 Institute for Labor and Mental Health. Reproduced by permission of the author.

Despair is better than disinterest, but it's paralyzing. Let's say we actually wanted to do something meaningful about global warming—about the biggest single threat that the entire earth has ever faced. We'd need, first, to understand a few things:

We need to transform our energy systems—renewable power, not coal, gas, and oil.

The Global Warming Challenge

It's coming at us fast. Our foremost climatologist, NASA's [the National Aeronautics and Space Administration's] James Hansen, said in the autumn of 2005 that his computer model, so far the world's most reliable, indicated that we had ten years to reverse the flow of carbon dioxide into the atmosphere or else we'd guarantee "a totally different planet," one where the stability of the Greenland and West Antarctic ice sheets could no longer be guaranteed. We're already facing, without immediate and dramatic change, huge temperature increases—the consensus estimate is about five degrees Fahrenheit this century, which would make the planet far warmer than any time during the age of primates, and do more harm to poor people, other species, and the fabric of life than anything short of an all-out nuclear exchange.

That means we need to transform our energy systems—renewable power, not coal, gas, and oil. That's a tall order (fossil fuels were a kind of magic—cheap, easy to find, easy to transport, loaded with BTUs) but it's only the beginning. The math makes clear that we also need to change the ways we live: stop sprawling, start taking trains; stop shipping our food 1,500 miles, start eating close to home.

We need to do this at the toughest possible moment— when the rest of the world, particularly the Chinese and the Indians, are finally starting to use fossil fuel in appreciable quantities. Not American quantities—we'll be the per capita champs for all time. But the rate of their growth, which is pulling people out of poverty, makes the math hard.

It's not impossible to square this circle. The biggest international panel of economists and engineers to look at the data concluded last spring that we had just enough time and just enough technology, and that the cost wouldn't break us: they suggested that the window was still open wide enough for us to squeeze through. But we've waited until the last possible second. Here's the consensus among those of us who have been working on this problem for two decades about what needs to happen, a consensus developed over the last year through a coalition called One Sky:

Our only hope is a movement, first in this country and then around the world.

Necessary Changes

First, the U.S. has to take the lead. We're the biggest source of the problem—it will be forty years before China's contribution to global warming matches what we've done in the course of our development. And for the last two decades we've blocked progress, even as the Europeans and the Japanese have tried to get the world mobilized. In the first few months of the next presidency [in 2009], we need a piece of comprehensive legislation that commits us to cutting carbon emissions 80 percent by 2050, that guarantees we'll stop building new coal-fired power plants, and that sets up a Green Jobs Corps to start actually making these changes. Tough, mandatory targets drive change.

Second, once we do that, we've got to get back in the international game. For many years now the U.S. and China (and now India) have used each other as convenient excuses for not taking action. If there's any hope at all, it will come from those three nations leading the negotiations for a grand global bargain—one that takes some of the wealth the West has built up in two oil-fueled centuries and uses it to subsidize the technologies the poor world needs to develop in a more durable fashion. It's actually fairly simple—everyone holds a knife to everyone else's throat right now, and we need to figure out how to drop them. And then we have to pick up wrenches, and get to work.

If you were placing bets, you'd be ill-advised to wager a whole lot that we'll get these two tasks accomplished. The vested interests are enormously strong (Exxon made more profit last year than any company in the history of profits). The inertia is even stronger (we like to fly in jets). That's why our only hope is a movement, first in this country and then around the world. This movement must possess at least as much moral urgency and willingness to sacrifice as the Civil Rights movement a generation ago. It's a movement that's unimaginable without leadership from people of faith.

It's starting. Last spring [2007] we organized 1,400 demonstrations in all fifty states on a single April day. We have the tools—the internet above all—that might let it spread virally. But it's going to take a kind of commitment we haven't yet approached. So screw in a new light bulb. And then screw in a new Congressperson. Drive a hybrid, sure, but drive change. Do it hard enough and you've earned the right to hope.

11

The Ethics of Reducing Global Warming Guilt

Iain Murray

Iain Murray is a member of the Church of England and works at the Competitive Enterprise Institute in Washington, D.C.

Recently, a faith-based organization designed a method for Christians to reduce guilt over global warming. First, the organization offers advice to help individuals reduce carbon dioxide emissions. Next, the organization offers an opportunity for individuals to pay a yearly fee ($99) that will be used to reduce carbon emissions. The money, theoretically, will cover the average person's carbon emissions per year (23 tons). In a sense, then, by paying a yearly fee, Christians who are worried about global warming can have a guilt-free conscience. Luckily for those promoting carbon trading, there are no federal regulations.

Are you a carbon-using Christian? Feeling guilty about all that carbon dioxide (CO_2) you pump into the atmosphere by such awful things as breathing, heating and cooling your home, lighting your work or study space, or driving to church? Now, like traditional sinners whose only mistake was breaking the Ten Commandments, you can atone for your carbon sins by buying carbon offsets from the Evangelical Climate Initiative—though I thought it was pre-Reformation Roman Catholicism, not Protestant evangelicalism, that endorsed indulgences.

Iain Murray, "A Pardoner's Tale," *American Spectator*, September 25, 2007, p. 6. Copyright © *The American Spectator* 2007. Reproduced by permission. www.cei.org/utils/printer.cfm?AID=6155.

The ECI now offers to help you expiate your carbon sins quickly and easily, online. (But wait; to go online, you must use your computer, which uses electricity, which probably is generated by burning coal or oil, which puts more carbon into the air. Might it be better to stay off the Web and pray instead?)

Absolving Carbon Emissions Sins

It's a simple, two-step process.

First, you go through a page that helps you "Do What You Can" by selecting simple actions you can promise to take now to reduce your carbon emissions in transportation, home, and society. There's no telling, of course, just by how much you'll reduce your emissions, because none of these actions is quantified. For example, you might volunteer to change your driving habits by accelerating and stopping more gradually, thus saving fuel. But how much more gradually? Five percent? Twenty? Thirty? Each will yield a different emission reduction—and it'll be impossible to know how much emission reduction you've achieved. Keep this in mind for later. As it happens, I already do two of the big things that will set me along the right path. Am I without sin? It doesn't appear so, as we'll find out.

Funny, my King James Bible doesn't mention that reducing my carbon emissions to zero is part of fulfilling Jesus' teaching to love my neighbors or be a steward of God's creation.

Secondly, you come to a page that offers you the opportunity to "Offset the Rest." Here's where the Evangelical Climate Initiative becomes the Medieval Catholic Indulgence Initiative.

The copy reads like one of those late-night TV infomercials punctuated with "But wait! There's more!":

After doing what you can, the second step is to pay us $99 per year to reduce your global warming pollution to zero. . . .

Your $99 contribution to the cause of helping to solve global warming is an investment in creating a better future for our children and those most vulnerable to the impacts of global warming. Reducing your emissions to zero is part of fulfilling Jesus' teaching to love our neighbors and be a proper steward of God's creation.

To do this we offset your emissions by reducing global warming pollution through contributions to energy efficiency projects, renewable energy projects, and reforestation projects. . . .

Funny, my King James Bible doesn't mention that reducing my carbon emissions to zero is part of fulfilling Jesus' teaching to love my neighbors or be a steward of God's creation. Just to be sure I wasn't missing something, I consulted a Concordance and did a search for the phrases "carbon emissions" and "carbon neutral." Strangely, I found neither. I couldn't even find the word "carbon." (I did find uses of the word "emission," in newer translations, but on a different subject entirely.) Maybe the ECI folks, in keeping with their infomercial ad approach, are using the "New! Improved! Expanded!" version of the Bible.

The True Cost of Carbon Emissions

But that's not all! (Oh, no, I've succumbed to the contagion!) How in God's creation can ECI know that $99 is going to be not too much, not too little, but just right to "offset the rest" of my carbon emissions if we couldn't quantify what my emissions were in the first place, or what the "Do What You Can" steps I chose to take would accomplish? Not to worry. ECI tells us that "The average American is responsible for about 23 tons of CO_2 pollution." And it just so happens that $99 (Not $78 or $103.54? How did it just happen to come to a price right under the $100 threshold past which consumers are much less likely to purchase?) is just enough to offset 23 tons of CO_2 per year—neither 22 tons nor 24, but the magic . . . er, I mean, very Christian, number 23.

ECI works all this out in partnership with carbonfund.org, which features a serious-looking, complicated way to figure out—eureka!—"exactly how much CO_2 you're responsible for." A sample—might it be based on something like an average?—suggests 16.11 tons of CO_2 for an individual, for which the offset cost is $88.61. That works out to a little more than $5.50 per ton. Multiplying that by 23 tons would give an offset price of $126.51, so apparently ECI is offering us a discount rate. I can hear it now: "But wait! Now, for a limited time only, you can get your 23-ton carbon offset for a discounted price of $99! You save $27.51, over 20 percent! Order now and we'll send you a set of Ginsu knives, absolutely free!"

But I Digress. We were wondering how ECI could know for certain that $99 would offset "the rest." Well, it turns out that ECI wants you to do a work of supererogation—above and beyond the requirements of its new, improved, and expanded version of the Word of God. After you "Do What You Can" to reduce your carbon emissions, you buy an indulgence sufficient to pay for all your carbon emissions before reduction! Presumably this leaves a treasury of merit that ECI can dole out to others. But I wouldn't hold my breath—though that would reduce my own CO_2 emissions—waiting for that, since that would diminish ECI's revenues from the project.

What I find most interesting is that I had previously worked out, using the EPA's emissions calculator, that carbon emissions for my entire family come to 30,502 lbs. of CO_2 per year. Carbonfund.org tells me that I only need to buy a $99 offset package if my individual emissions are over 50,715 lbs for the year. Using carbonfund's own $5.50-per-metric-ton figure, it turns out I'm not getting a discount, I'm being overcharged by ECI for about $20. Is this hypererogation?

A Clean, Green Conscience

ECI doesn't mention that while the average American is responsible for 23 tons of CO_2 emissions per year, Al Gore's Nashville house—he's got others—uses 20 times as much electricity as the average American's home. Maybe ECI can get Gore to buy his carbon offsets from them? Sorry. That won't happen. Gore is part owner of his own carbon offsets and trading companies and gets his offsets as part of his benefits package. ECI isn't the only party with something to gain from scaring people about global warming.

Be all that as it may, having read through the "Offset the Rest" page you come to the button to "Purchase your offset now."

The next page offers you various levels of donation—not purchase, mind you, this is pure donation, though it does buy you a clean, green conscience—ranging from the still-rankling minimum of $99 to the princely sum of $1,099—and then, for students, $25. (So that's what they do with the excess merits from the works of supererogation by all those saints who offset more CO_2 than they emit!) You even have the opportunity to make this a recurring donation every year, quarter, or month. Then you can choose the types of offsets you want to buy—renewable energy, energy efficiency, or reforestation. Finally, you fill in your personal details, and give ECI your credit card information.

Needless to say, I didn't pony up the money. So when I clicked "Cancel" instead, a page came up that told me "There was an error processing your step 2 payment. This step has not yet been completed." Oh yes, it has!

The Free Market and Carbon Trading

One last concern: Where's the Good Housekeeping seal of approval on ECI's moneymaking site? Or the Better Business Bureau logo? Or the link to information about how the Securities and Exchange Commission regulates the carbon offsets and carbon trading businesses to make sure there's no monkey business going on? They're not there, because—well, because there is no regulation of this business. Apparently the ECI has finally found a tiny bit of the free market that it doesn't want to strangle with regulation. One wonders, though, what happened to the ECI's strong suspicion of sin in every branch of the corporate world. Or is the carbon offset industry impeccable?

It appears to me that this particular branch of evangelical theology is in dire need of a reformation. When it comes to the sin of carbon emission, perhaps carbon-using Christians should remember the words of Martin Luther's Letter to Melanchthon: "Be a sinner and sin strongly, but more strongly have faith and rejoice in Christ."

12

Greenhouse Gases Negatively Impact the Environment

National Resources Defense Council

The National Resources Defense Council is an environmental action organization.

Global warming is having an adverse effect in the Artic regions. Ice shelves that have been in existence for 3,000 years are breaking up, and the changing climate is negatively impacting polar wildlife (bears, walruses, whales, and seals). Melting glaciers will contribute to rising sea levels, leading to more flooding in low-lying areas. Global warming will also disrupt food production (especially wheat) around the world. While the consequences are dire, global warming can be controlled if we conserve energy and reduce our reliance on fossil fuels.

1. *Why are global warming specialists watching the Arctic so closely?*

The Arctic is global warming's canary in the coal mine. It's a highly sensitive region, and it's being profoundly affected by the changing climate. Most scientists view what's happening now in the Arctic as a harbinger of things to come.

2. *What kinds of changes are taking place in the Arctic now?*

Average temperatures in the Arctic region are rising twice as fast as they are elsewhere in the world. Arctic ice is getting thinner, melting and rupturing. For example, the largest single block of ice in the Arctic, the Ward Hunt Ice Shelf, had been around for 3,000 years before it started cracking in 2000. Within two years it had split all the way through and is now breaking into pieces.

The polar ice cap as a whole is shrinking. Images from NASA [National Aeronautics and Space Administration] satellites show that the area of permanent ice cover is contracting at a rate of 9 percent each decade. If this trend continues, summers in the Arctic could become ice-free by the end of the century.

3. *How does this dramatic ice melt affect the Arctic?*

The melting of once-permanent ice is already affecting native people, wildlife and plants. When the Ward Hunt Ice Shelf splintered, the rare freshwater lake it enclosed, along with its unique ecosystem, drained into the ocean. Polar bears, whales, walrus and seals are changing their feeding and migration patterns, making it harder for native people to hunt them. And along Arctic coastlines, entire villages will be uprooted because they're in danger of being swamped. The native people of the Arctic view global warming as a threat to their cultural identity and their very survival.

4. *Will Arctic ice melt have any effects beyond the polar region?*

Yes—the contraction of the Arctic ice cap is accelerating global warming. Snow and ice usually form a protective, cooling layer over the Arctic. When that covering melts, the earth absorbs more sunlight and gets hotter. And the latest scientific data confirm the far-reaching effects of climbing global temperatures.

Melting glaciers and land-based ice sheets also contribute to rising sea levels.

Rising temperatures are already affecting Alaska, where the spruce bark beetle is breeding faster in the warmer weather.

These pests now sneak in an extra generation each year. From 1993 to 2003, they chewed up 3.4 million acres of Alaskan forest.

Melting glaciers and land based ice sheets also contribute to rising sea levels, threatening low-lying areas around the globe with beach erosion, coastal flooding, and contamination of freshwater supplies. (Sea level is not affected when floating sea ice melts.) At particular risk are island nations like the Maldives; over half of that nation's populated islands lie less than 6 feet above sea level. Even major cities like Shanghai and Lagos would face similar problems, as they also lie just six feet above present water levels.

Rising seas would severely impact the United States as well. Scientists project as much as a 3-foot sea-level rise by 2100. According to a 2001 U.S. Environmental Protection Agency study, this increase would inundate some 22,400 square miles of land along the Atlantic and Gulf coasts of the United States, primarily in Louisiana, Texas, Florida and North Carolina.

A warmer Arctic will also affect weather patterns and thus food production around the world. Wheat farming in Kansas, for example, would be profoundly affected by the loss of ice cover in the Arctic. According to a NASA Goddard Institute of Space Studies computer model, Kansas would be 4 degrees warmer in the winter without Arctic ice, which normally creates cold air masses that frequently slide southward into the United States. Warmer winters are bad news for wheat farmers, who need freezing temperatures to grow winter wheat. And in summer, warmer days would rob Kansas soil of 10 percent of its moisture, drying out valuable cropland.

5. *Can we do anything to stop global warming?*

Yes. When we burn fossil fuels—oil, coal and gas—to generate electricity and power our vehicles, we produce the heat-trapping gases that cause global warming. The more we burn, the faster churns the engine of global climate change. Thus the most important thing we can do is save energy.

And we *can* do it. Technologies exist today to make cars that run cleaner and burn less gas, generate electricity from wind and sun, modernize power plants, and build refrigerators, air conditioners and whole buildings that use less power. As individuals, each of us can take steps to save energy and fight global warming.

13

Greenhouse Gases Do Not Negatively Impact the Environment

Lorne Gunter

Lorne Gunter is a senior columnist at the Edmonton Journal.

Saturn and Pluto, like Earth, have warmed in recent years. While a consensus has formed around the connection between human-generated greenhouse gases and global warming, there are no human-generated greenhouse gases on Saturn and Pluto. A handful of scientists, however, have proposed a simpler cause: the sun. For the last 100 years or so, increased solar activity has warmed the planet, just as it has in the past. Once this active solar phase ends in 20 to 40 years, Earth will once again start to cool.

Mars's ice caps are melting, and Jupiter is developing a second giant red spot, an enormous hurricane-like storm.

The existing Great Red Spot is 300 years old and twice the size of Earth. The new storm—Red Spot Jr.—is thought to be the result of a sudden warming on our solar system's largest planet. Dr. Imke de Pater of Berkeley University says some parts of Jupiter are now as much as six degrees Celsius warmer than just a few years ago.

Neptune's moon, Triton, studied in 1989 after the unmanned Voyageur probe flew past, seems to have heated up significantly since then. Parts of its frozen nitrogen surface have begun melting and turning to gas, making Triton's atmosphere denser.

Even Pluto has warmed slightly in recent years, if you can call −230C instead of −233C "warmer."

And I swear, I haven't left my SUV idling on any of those planets or moons. Honest, I haven't.

Is there something all these heavenly bodies have in common? Some one thing they all share that could be causing them to warm in unison?

The Sun and Global Warming

Hmmm, is there some giant, self-luminous ball of burning gas with a mass more than 300,000 times that of Earth and a core temperature of more than 20-million degrees Celsius, that for the past century or more has been unusually active and powerful? Is there something like that around which they all revolve that could be causing this multi-globe warming? Naw!

They must all have congested commuter highways, coal-fired power plants and oilsands developments that are releasing large amounts of carbon dioxide into their atmospheres, too.

A decade ago, when global warming and Kyoto [an international environmental accord] was just beginning to capture public attention, I published a quiz elsewhere that bears repeating in our current hyper-charged environmental debate: Quick, which is usually warmer, day or night?

And what is typically the warmest part of the day? The warmest time of year?

Finally, which are generally warmer: cloudy or cloudless days?

If you answered day, afternoon, summer and cloudless you may be well on your way to understanding what is causing global warming.

For the past century and a half, Earth has been warming. Coincidentally (or perhaps not so coincidentally), during that same period, our sun has been brightening, becoming more active, sending out more radiation.

Habibullah Abdussamatov of the Pulkovo Astronomical Observatory in St. Petersburg, Sami Solanki of the Max Planck Institute for Solar System Research in Germany, Sallie Baliunas and Willie Soon of the Solar and Stellar Physics Division of the Harvard-Smithsonian Center for Astrophysics and a host of the rest of the world's leading solar scientists are all convinced that the warming of recent years is not unusual and that nearly all the warming in the past 150 years can be attributed to the sun.

The sun's current active phase is expected to wane in 20 to 40 years, at which time the planet will begin cooling.

The History of Climate Change

Solar scientists from Iowa to Siberia have overlaid the last several warm periods on our planet with known variations in our sun's activity and found, according to Mr. Solanki, "a near-perfect match."

Mr. Abdussamatov concedes manmade gases may have made "a small contribution to the warming in recent years, but it cannot compete with the increase in solar irradiance."

Mr. Soon showed as long ago as the mid-1990s that the depth of the Little Ice Age—the coldest period in the northern hemisphere in the past 1,500 years—corresponded perfectly with a solar event known as the Maunder Minimum. For nearly seven decades there was virtually no sunspot activity.

Our sun was particularly quiet. And for those 60 to 70 years, the northern half of our globe, at least, was in a deep freeze.

Is it so hard to believe then that the sun could be causing our current warming, too?

At the very least, the fact that so many prominent scientists have legitimate, logical objections to the current global warming orthodoxy means there is no "consensus" among scientists about the cause.

Here's a prediction: The sun's current active phase is expected to wane in 20 to 40 years, at which time the planet will begin cooling. Since that is when most of the greenhouse emission reductions proposed by the UN and others are slated to come into full effect, the "greens" will see that cooling and claim, "See, we warned you and made you take action, and look, we saved the planet."

Of course, they will have had nothing to do with it.

14

Curbing Greenhouse Gases Is Possible with Technological Solutions

Pew Center on Global Climate Change

The Pew Center works to bring together business leaders, policy makers, and scientists to form a new approach to environmental issues.

In order to prevent the worst effects of global warming, drastic changes will need to be made in how we consume energy. Fortunately, technologies are now available that can help reduce our reliance on fossil fuels and reduce the harm caused by the fossil fuels we continue to consume. In order for these new technologies to be economically feasible, however, new policies and incentives will be needed. The first set of technological solutions will be applied to the use of electricity; the second set, to transportation. In both cases, the combination of new energy sources (e.g., solar panels, ethanol fuel) and greater efficiency will work together to reduce carbon emissions. In transportation, there will need to be short-term solutions (more stringent emissions policies, corn-based ethanol) and long-term solutions (electric cars). To greatly reduce our reliance on fossil fuels, we will need to rely on multiple technologies and multiple solutions.

A chieving the 50- to 80-percent reduction in greenhouse gas emissions that scientists say is needed to avoid the worst effects of climate change will not be easy. It will require

Pew Center on Global Climate Change "Climate Change 101: Technological Solutions," *pewclimate.org*, 2008, p. 11. Reproduced by permission. www.pewclimate.org.

action across all sectors of the economy, from electricity and transportation to agriculture. Cost-effective opportunities exist today for starting the world on a path toward lower emissions—and there are a number of emerging technologies that hold enormous promise for delivering substantial emission reductions in the future. The successful development of these technologies will require substantial new investments in research, incentives for producers and consumers, and emission reduction requirements that drive innovation. Governments at all levels need to encourage short-term action to reduce emissions while laying the groundwork for a longer-term technology revolution.

The Dawning of a Revolution

The greenhouse gas (GHG) emissions that are causing global warming come from a wide range of sources, including cars and trucks, power plants, farms, and more. . . . Because there are so many sources of these gases, there are also many options for reducing emissions, including such readily available steps as improving energy efficiency and changing industrial processes and agricultural practices.

Most importantly, the world needs to fundamentally change the way it produces and consumes energy.

However, seriously addressing global climate change will require a decades-long commitment to develop and deploy new, low-GHG technologies around the world. Most importantly, the world needs to fundamentally change the way it produces and consumes energy. The global population is rising fast; in developing and developed countries alike, population and income growth means more people are using more energy, driving more cars and trucks, and building more homes.

Without a revolution in energy technology, human societies will be pumping ever-increasing amounts of greenhouse gases into the atmosphere, with potentially dramatic effects on the global climate. The time to begin making the necessary investments in new technologies is right now.

Achieving substantial reductions in greenhouse gas emissions is possible—now and in the decades to come. Some emissions-reducing technologies (such as hybrid gas-electric cars and wind power) are commercially competitive today. Others (such as plug-in hybrid cars and solar power) are on their way. And still more (such as hydrogen fuel cells and storing carbon dioxide emissions underground) show great promise, but additional work is needed to demonstrate their effectiveness and cost-effectiveness.

There is no single, silver-bullet technology that will deliver the reductions in emissions that are needed to protect the climate.

New Policies and Incentives

Almost all of these technologies are going to need help moving from the laboratory to the marketplace. Right now, the true "costs" of greenhouse gas emissions are not reflected in the marketplace, meaning there is little incentive for producers or consumers to reduce their contribution to the climate problem. In addition to policies that send a clear "price signal" by placing real limits on emissions, governments will need to invest in research to develop some of the most critical, long-term, climate friendly technologies and to ensure that they can gain a solid foothold in the marketplace. Consumers and businesses also need government incentives to purchase these technologies so they can enter the mainstream and contribute to substantial reductions in emissions.

Opponents of strong action to address climate change often focus on the economic costs of reducing emissions. Yes, massive investments are needed. But the cost of inaction is even greater. In addition, a global technology revolution will create enormous economic opportunities for businesses and workers, as well as the localities and states that successfully position themselves as centers of innovation and technology development for a low-carbon world.

There is no single, silver-bullet technology that will deliver the reductions in emissions that are needed to protect the climate. Success will require a portfolio of solutions, many of which are available today. Looking across key sectors of the economy, it is possible to identify those technologies that may help the most. For policymakers, the priority must be to create incentives that will unleash the power of the marketplace to develop solutions, rather than to pick technologies based on predictions of future performance. . . .

Most greenhouse gas emissions in the United States can be traced to the electricity, building and transportation sectors. The following pages look at technology options for reducing emissions from each of these critical sectors.

Electricity and Buildings

The electricity sector produces 38 percent of U.S. carbon dioxide emissions. Most of the electricity generated by the sector is used in the nation's homes, offices and industrial structures to power everything from heating and cooling systems to lights, computers, refrigerators and cell phones.

This massive use of electricity is not the only way in which buildings contribute to climate change. Non-electrical energy sources such as natural gas furnaces also produce greenhouse gases on their own.

Because they make such a significant contribution to the problem, the electricity and building sectors also can play a crucial role in solutions to climate change. Reducing emissions from these closely related sectors requires looking at both electric power and building technology options. In other words, it's important to think about the roles of both the producers and the consumers of power.

> *Technologies are available today to produce electric power and heat more efficiently using both fossil fuels and renewable energy.*

Electric Power Options Greenhouse gas emissions from the electric power sector come primarily from power plants burning coal or natural gas. Options for reducing these emissions include:

Improved Efficiency. Technologies are available today to produce electric power and heat more efficiently using both fossil fuels and renewable energy. Power plants using the Integrated Gasification and Combined Cycle (IGCC) process, for example, deliver efficiency gains along with reductions in air pollution by converting coal into a cleaner-burning gas. Additional efficiency gains can come from advanced technologies for other fuel sources in power plants, including natural gas and biomass.

Renewable Energy. Renewable energy harnesses the power of the wind, the sun, water, tides and other forces to produce electric power. Agricultural "biomass" products also can be used to generate electricity and heat when combusted with coal. Renewables offer the potential to generate electricity without producing greenhouse gases—or producing very little when compared to traditional energy sources. Most renewable resources can be harnessed on a large-scale basis (for example, via wind farms or large geothermal fields) or in more "distributed" forms (for example, by placing solar panels on rooftops). Although larger-scale renewable energy can be cost-competitive with other forms of conventional electricity in some cases, renewables still count for only a tiny share of overall electricity generation in the United States. Options for expanding the use of renewables include Renewable Portfolio Standards, which require generators to produce a specified share of power from renewable sources; consumer rebates and other government incentives; and further support for research and development to advance the technologies and lower their costs.

Carbon Capture and Sequestration. As noted above, IGCC power plants can convert coal into a gas that produces substantially fewer pollutants when burned; the IGCC process also allows for the relatively easy "capture" of carbon for long-term storage in underground geological formations. The United States has built demonstration plants using these technologies, and at least one commercial IGCC plant is being planned. But the overwhelming majority of coal-burning power plants in the United States are conventional plants, and more work is needed to provide power producers with the incentives to build cleaner burning power plants as soon as possible, and to bring down the costs of capturing carbon from conventional coal plants. Work also is needed to prove that underground storage (or sequestration) of carbon on a large scale is a good long-term option for keeping it out of the atmosphere.

Cost-effective technologies for reducing emissions from buildings are readily available, but they often can't compete in the marketplace.

Nuclear Power. Nuclear power currently provides roughly 20 percent of U.S. electricity with virtually no associated greenhouse gas emissions. Yet, for nuclear power to play a more prominent role in U.S. efforts to address climate change, the industry needs to overcome several important hurdles. These include concerns among citizens and elected officials about the cost of nuclear-generated electricity; technical, political and environmental concerns about nuclear waste disposal; and threats associated with increased risk of nuclear arms proliferation. No new nuclear plant has been ordered in the United States since 1979, although groups of companies are currently pursuing applications for new plants.

Options for Buildings Greenhouse gas emissions from the building sector result primarily from the use of power-hungry items such as lighting fixtures, appliances, and heating and cooling systems. Cost-effective technologies for reducing emissions from buildings are readily available, but they often can't compete in the marketplace. Among the reasons are a lack of consumer information, and "market barriers" such as the high fees that electric utilities often charge for back-up power to customers using their own sources of energy.

Because of inefficiencies in how power is generated and reaches consumers, reductions in demand by energy users result in even larger energy savings by the generator. Options for reducing emissions from buildings include encouraging greater energy efficiency and promoting on-site power generation.

> *Efficiency.* There are many ways to increase the overall energy efficiency of buildings. From more efficient lighting and instantaneous hot water heaters to EnergyStar®-certified products and better insulation, consumers and businesses have an array of cost-effective options for limiting their energy use and boosting efficiency. However, consumers often do not take advantage of these options on their own. Policymakers can help promote greater energy efficiency through enhanced building codes; building standards, awards or certifications to buildings that are energy-efficient; suspended sales taxes on efficient appliances; publicly funded utility efficiency programs; regulatory reforms that reduce barriers to energy efficiency; appliance standards and labeling; and other steps.

> *On-site Power Generation.* Greenhouse gas emissions from the electricity and building sectors also can be reduced through on-site power generation using renewables and

other climate-friendly energy resources. Examples include rooftop solar panels, solar water heating, small-scale wind generation, stationary fuel cells powered by natural gas or renewable hydrogen and geothermal heat-pumps. While the costs for all of these options are falling, some of the technologies remain fairly expensive and thus are not widely used in the marketplace. Expanding their use—which will ultimately reduce costs—may require new incentive programs such as consumer rebates and tax credits. Building standards (such as LEED™-certification) also can help. In addition, combined heat-and-power (or cogeneration) plants, rather than wasting the excess heat generated in the course of producing electricity, capture it for use in heating homes and industrial sites. Many of these technologies already are cost-effective, but they can't compete in the market because of regulatory hurdles and other barriers.

Historically, it has proven very hard to get people to drive less.

Transportation

After the electricity or buildings sector, transportation is the second largest source of greenhouse gas emissions in the United States, primarily carbon dioxide produced by cars and trucks. The ways in which we move from place to place are responsible for almost one-third of U.S. carbon dioxide emissions, and nearly a quarter of emissions around the world.

Reducing greenhouse gas emissions from transportation can be accomplished in a number of ways. Among the options:

- Adopting new emissions-reducing technologies for cars and trucks;

- Reducing the carbon content of vehicle fuels; and

- Reducing demand for vehicle travel by encouraging "smart growth" and the use of mass transit.

Historically, it has proven very hard to get people to drive less. The way most Americans live today, our cars and trucks are an essential part of our daily lives. There are ways to make Americans less automobile-dependent and new options such as car-sharing and smart growth are emerging.

The challenge for lawmakers at all levels is to promote and encourage short-term solutions (for example, more hybrid cars and trucks) while facilitating a long-term transition to alternatively-fueled vehicles.

Short-Term Options for Transportation

Significant reductions in greenhouse gas emissions from conventional cars and trucks are possible through the use of "off-the-shelf" technologies that are commercially available today. One recent study found that commercial (and cost-effective) technologies exist right now to increase fuel economy and/or reduce tailpipe greenhouse gas emissions by as much as 25 percent.

In the United States, however, the average fuel economy of all cars and light trucks sold today is no better than it was in the early 1980s. . . . Governments around the world have adopted more stringent policies than the United States to reduce tailpipe greenhouse gas emissions and/or increase fuel economy. These policies can play a crucial role in hastening the rollout of commercially available technology to reduce vehicle emissions.

Another option for reducing greenhouse gas emissions from cars and trucks in the short term is the blending of ethanol and other biologically-derived fuels with gasoline. Ethanol derived from corn is currently the dominant biofuel in the United States. Depending on how it is produced and processed, corn-based ethanol can yield reductions of as much as 30 percent in emissions for each gallon of regular gasoline that it replaces. Other biofuels that can be developed over the longer term promise to deliver significantly larger reductions (see below).

Beyond these "off-the-shelf" options for reducing car and truck emissions, even greater reductions are available through the use of advanced diesel and hybrid vehicle technologies.

Diesels and hybrids use different engines than the standard internal combustion engine; diesels also use different fuels. The key advantage of these technologies is that they both offer significant improvements in fuel economy. Because hybrid and diesel vehicles use less gas on a per-mile basis, they produce fewer greenhouse gas emissions when compared to other cars and trucks. When both technologies are combined in a diesel hybrid vehicle, it can yield a 65-percent reduction in greenhouse gas emissions per mile.

Longer-Term Options for Transportation

Ultimately, reducing greenhouse gas emissions from cars and trucks to a level where they pose a minimal risk to the climate will require a shift away from petroleum-based fuels. Among the most promising alternatives: running cars and trucks on electricity, next-generation biofuels or hydrogen.

> *Biofuels.* Agricultural sources can be used to produce transportation fuel. While ethanol currently produced in the United States comes from corn, the technology exists to make biofuels from "cellulosic" sources (or the woody and leafy parts of plants). While corn-based ethanol can reduce emissions by as much as 30 percent for every gallon of traditional fuel replaced, cellulosic ethanol and sugar-cane based ethanol may enable reductions of up to 100 percent. (This is because any emissions produced through the use of these fuels could be offset as farmers grow more carbon-dioxide-consuming biofuel crops.) Biofuels have the potential to offset 10 to 24 percent of current U.S. greenhouse gas emissions, depending on what fossil fuels are replaced and

on how the agricultural product is converted into fuels. Another biofuel option is biodiesel, which can be produced from a wide range of oilseed crops (such as soybeans or palm and cotton seeds) and can be used to replace diesel fuel. With ethanol from sugar cane providing almost half of its domestic passenger fuel, Brazil has shown that an aggressive policy push can help biofuels become a mainstream fuel choice.

Electric Cars. Historically, electric cars have been viewed as a "niche" product, but advances in battery storage are needed. Another option is the "plug-in" hybrid, a gas-electric vehicle that can be charged at home overnight. Even using the current U.S. mix of electricity sources to charge the vehicles, plug-in hybrids can achieve significant reductions in greenhouse gas emissions compared to traditional vehicles, and even traditional hybrids.

Hydrogen. Hydrogen fuel cells, long a staple of the U.S. space program, produce power by combining oxygen with hydrogen to create water. Technological advances and reductions in the costs associated with the use of fuel cells could lay the groundwork for a hydrogen-based transportation system in the decades to come. However, a number of issues still need to be resolved before fuel cells can deliver on the promise of offering a "zero-emission" transportation solution. Among the most important questions: how to produce hydrogen in ways that yield minimal emissions.

To achieve significant reductions in U.S. greenhouse gas emissions, our nation needs to embrace short-term and long-term solutions.

Combining Technologies

To achieve significant reductions in U.S. greenhouse gas emissions, our nation needs to embrace short-term and long-term solutions. We need to target both supply and demand—engaging consumers and producers of energy in a wide-ranging effort to protect the climate. And we need broad policies aimed at curbing emissions, together with more targeted policies designed to spur the development of new technologies.

Encouraging greater energy efficiency is a crucial part of the solution. Throughout all sectors of the U.S. economy, gains in energy efficiency can make an important contribution to reducing greenhouse gas emissions—and, in turn, reducing the amount of power needed from new and emerging low-carbon energy sources. One group of experts found that if the United States can boost energy efficiency by 2 percent per year through 2050, we will reduce the amount of power needed from low-carbon sources by two-thirds. Clearly, efficiency across all sectors is essential, both as a path to short-term reductions in emissions and as part of a long-term strategy as well.

Also essential will be a wide-ranging effort to drive innovation. Government at all levels needs to spur investments in new technologies—by making direct investments in research and development, creating and enhancing incentives for private investment, and adopting mandatory targets and other policies that can help create the conditions for technological change.

Relying on Multiple Solutions

Among the key climate solutions advocated by many experts is a "cap-and-trade" system that requires emissions reductions while allowing companies to trade emission credits so they can achieve their reductions as cost-effectively as possible. The most important benefit of such an approach is that it establishes a value for emissions reductions, as well as an economic advantage for technologies that can achieve them.

Coupled with government efforts to promote the development and deployment of new technologies, cap-and-trade programs hold the promise of encouraging climate solutions without threatening the competitiveness of U.S. industry.

In order to successfully reduce the threat of climate change, the United States and other nations will have to rely on a wide range of technologies over the next century. The exact portfolio of technologies that will be required to achieve the necessary emission reductions is not clear. What is clear, however, is that policies are going to be needed to aid in the development of new technological solutions and to move many of these technologies into the marketplace.

Given the national and global implications of climate change and efforts to address it, leadership from the federal government on these issues is going to be crucial. At the same time, state and local leaders have jurisdiction over many parts of the economy that are part of the problem—and that can be part of the solution as well. These leaders will play a key role in the search for solutions, and in making sure that communities across the country can benefit from the technology revolution that is needed to deliver a low-carbon future.

15

Carbon Taxes, Not Carbon Caps, Can Reduce Greenhouse Gases

Economist

Economist *is a weekly newspaper.*

In an attempt to curb greenhouse gases, many countries have adopted cap-and-trade systems, systems that allow a central authority to set carbon emission limits (represented by issued permits) for individual companies. When a company exceeds the limit, it must buy more permits. Unfortunately, the system is ineffective. If the number of permits is under or overestimated, prices for permits will be either too high or too low, causing economic volatility. Furthermore, cap-and-trade systems offer few incentives for technological innovation. Carbon taxes, on the other hand, would create a more efficient system that could be easily adjusted if miscalculated. The taxes would also create revenue that could help support businesses affected by higher fuel costs. Unfortunately, the idea of creating a new tax is politically difficult, even though a carbon tax, in the end, would work better economically.

Tradable emissions permits are a popular, but inferior, way to tackle global warming

The pressure for political action on climate change has never looked stronger. Even [President] George [W.] Bush has now joined the leaders of other rich countries in their quest to negotiate a successor regime to the Kyoto protocol [an international environmental accord] treaty on curbing greenhouse gases that expires in 2012.

Too bad, then, that politicians seem set on a second-best route to a greener world. That is the path of cap-and-trade, where the quantity of emissions is limited (the cap) and the right to emit is distributed through a system of tradable permits. The original Kyoto treaty set up such a mechanism and its signatories are keen to expand it. The main market-based alternative—a carbon tax—has virtually no political support.

A pity, because most economists agree that carbon taxes are a better way to reduce greenhouse gases than cap-and-trade schemes. That is because taxes deal more efficiently than do permits with the uncertainty surrounding carbon control. In the neat world of economic theory, carbon reduction makes sense until the marginal cost of cutting carbon emissions is equal to the marginal benefit of cutting carbon emissions. If policymakers knew the exact shape of these cost and benefit curves, it would matter little whether they reached this optimal level by targeting the quantity of emissions (through a cap) or setting the price (through a tax).

Cap-and-trade schemes cause unnecessary economic damage because the price of permits can be volatile.

But in the real world, politicians are fumbling in the dark. And that fumbling favours a tax. If policymakers set a carbon tax too low, too much carbon will be emitted. But since the environmental effect of greenhouse gases builds up over time, a temporary excess will make little difference to the overall path of global warming. Before much damage is done to the environment, the carbon tax can be raised.

Misjudging the number of permits, in contrast, could send permit prices either skywards or through the floor, with immediate, and costly, economic consequences. Worse, a fixed allotment of permits makes no adjustment for the business cycle (firms produce and pollute less during a recession).

The Limits of Cap-and-Trade Systems

Cap-and-trade schemes cause unnecessary economic damage because the price of permits can be volatile. Both big cap-and-trade schemes in existence today—Europe's Emissions-Trading Scheme for carbon and America's market for trading sulphur-dioxide permits (to reduce acid rain)—suggest this volatility can be acute. America has had tradable permits for SO_2 since the mid-1990s. Their price has varied, on average, by more than 40% a year. Given carbon's importance in the economy, similar fluctuations could significantly affect everything from inflation to consumer spending. Extreme price volatility might also deter people from investing in green technology.

Even without the volatility, some economists reckon that a cap-and-trade system produces fewer incentives than a carbon tax for climate-friendly innovation. A tax provides a clear price floor for carbon and hence a minimum return for any innovation. Under a cap-and-trade system, in contrast, an invention that reduced the cost of cutting carbon emissions could itself push down the price of permits, reducing investors' returns.

To avoid these pitfalls, some cap-and-trade advocates want to set price floors and ceilings within carbon-trading systems. One of the most prominent bills in America's Congress, for instance, includes a "safety valve". If the price of carbon rises beyond a threshold, the government will allocate an unlimited supply of permits at that price. Such reforms, in effect, make a cap-and-trade system work more like a carbon tax.

A third advantage of carbon taxes is that they raise revenue. Governments can use this cash to reduce other inefficient taxes, thereby cutting the economic costs of carbon abatement. Or they can use the money to compensate those, such as the poor, who are hit disproportionately hard by higher fuel costs.

The Great Green Giveaway

Cap-and-trade schemes, in contrast, have traditionally given away permits, which leaves no room to reduce the economic costs of climate control by cutting taxes elsewhere. But here, too, change may be afoot. To mimic the advantage of a carbon tax, many cap-and-trade fans now want governments to auction at least a share of the permits.

Too many politicians pretend that carbon taxes will hurt consumers more than a cap-and-trade scheme.

All of which raises an important question. If cap-and-trade schemes are to be reformed so that they look more like carbon taxes, why are politicians so reluctant to impose carbon taxes in the first place? One reason is that their environmental benefits are harder to explain. It is intuitively easier to grasp how a carbon cap will slow global warming. Taxes are also more prone to ideological caricature, particularly in America, where many conservatives argue instinctively that all taxes are bad. Too many politicians pretend that carbon taxes will hurt consumers more than a cap-and-trade scheme, even though the cost of carbon permits will be passed on to consumers just as quickly as a tax.

But the biggest problem, at least politically, is that carbon taxes are transparent and simple, whereas cap-and-trade systems are complicated and conveniently opaque. Under a cap-and-trade scheme, governments can pay off politically powerful polluters (such as the coal industry) by giving them permits. Even more important, rich countries can pay poorer ones to cut their emissions without any cash changing hands between governments. Under a carbon tax such transfers must go through the government's budget. And that can be politically tricky. However sensible it sounds to an economist, American voters may be loth to see their tax dollars funding fat cheques for China. Add in these political arguments and the choice between a carbon tax and cap-and-trade becomes less obvious. Politicians are heading down the second-best path to combat climate change, but it may be the only one that leads anywhere.

16

The Removal of Greenhouse Gases Will Require Practical Solutions

Brad Lemley

Brad Lemley writes for Discover *magazine.*

While a number of technological ideas have been suggested to curb carbon dioxide emissions, none have offered realistic solutions. One method that may hold promise, however, proposes that carbon dioxide can be removed directly from the atmosphere. Scientist Klaus Lackner is currently working on just such a solution, developing a synthetic tree. Each tree would remove 90,000 tons of carbon dioxide from the atmosphere each year, or the equivalent of the carbon dioxide generated by 15,000 cars per year. While certain aspects of the procedure are still problematic, Lackner believes it will offer a more efficient method for reducing carbon dioxide than comparative plans.

Wallace Broecker, Newberry Professor of Earth and Environmental Sciences at Columbia University, has some advice for global warming activists to follow over the next 100 years or so: Get real. Ecologists, he argues, have wrongly focused on developing power-generating technologies that don't use fossil fuels and don't spew carbon dioxide, which can trap solar radiation and warm the planet. "But we are a very long way from being able to get 30 or 40 percent of our energy from solar power," Broecker says. "If we bank on that, and it does not happen, we will be stuck." In his view, no carbon-free technology—including nuclear, wind, geothermal, and tidal—is likely to be deployed quickly enough to head off increasing accumulations of the greenhouse gas.

Even if easy-to-access oil begins to run out in a few years, as some geologists predict, Broecker says nations will simply switch to other relatively cheap fossil fuels. "The Athabasca tar sands in Canada are being mined and converted to petroleum at a cost of about $20 a barrel," he says. As long as oil prices remain at more than $50 a barrel, that's irresistibly profitable. "The next step would be to make petroleum out of coal, much like the Nazis did in World War II when their supply was cut off. It might double the price of gasoline, but that would still be cheaper than other alternate forms of energy."

There is simply no realistic way to clamp down on carbon-generating technologies before they fill the skies with high levels of carbon dioxide.

Broecker adds that what the developed wealthy world will do is largely irrelevant, because China, India, and much of the third world will grow increasingly wealthy and thirsty for fossil-fueled growth. "Since there are a billion and a half of us, and 5 billion people in the poorer parts of the world, it is more what they do to increase their fossil-fuel usage than what we do to decrease that matters," he says.

In short, there is simply no realistic way to clamp down on carbon-generating technologies before they fill the skies with high levels of carbon dioxide. Atmospheric CO_2, measured in parts per million, has been climbing steadily for more than 150 years and threatens to keep doing so. "We are headed toward 900 parts per million early in the next century," or more than double the current level of 380 ppm, Broecker says. "That would mean four to five Fahrenheit degrees of warming for the world as a whole, raising sea levels by a meter or more." And it won't stop there, he says. Sea levels might eventually even rise five meters, submerging the world's low-lying lands, including most of Florida.

Water vapor is the most potent greenhouse gas.

Removing CO_2 from the Atmosphere

The answer? "We need to work out a way to take CO_2 out of the air and bury it," Broecker says. He points to Klaus Lackner, a Columbia University geophysicist, and Alan Wright, an engineer formerly with the Biosphere 2 project, who are designing and building the first atmospheric CO_2 extraction machine. Gary Comer, founder of the Lands' End clothing company, is funding the project. Although he won't divulge exact figures, Broecker says "the cost of development is peanuts. If it turns out that the models that predict warming are not right, we can leave the technology on the shelf. But if we need it, it will be there."

A SIMPLE MOLECULE'S TANGLED TALE

Carbon dioxide, a gas made up of one carbon atom and two oxygen atoms, seems like an insignificant part of Earth's atmosphere. In 2004 it constituted just .038 percent by volume. But based on data gleaned from ice-core samples, the level of concentration is higher than it has been for 420,000 years. Many scientists think that increasing amounts of carbon dioxide and other gases in the atmosphere, much of which are attributable to human activity, trap solar radiation and slowly warm the planet. The theory is supported by the U.N.'s Intergovernmental Panel on Climate Change, the National Academy of Sciences, and other major scientific organizations. Detractors argue that Earth has warmed and cooled naturally for millennia and that the warming trend we are experiencing is unrelated to human activity.

STEAM HEAT

Water vapor is the most potent greenhouse gas. Atmospheric warming caused by CO_2 and other gases produced by fossil-fuel combustion heats the oceans' surface and boosts humidity, putting more water vapor into the air. In some models, the added moisture triples the warming effect of fossil fuels.

About 40 percent of the carbon added to the atmosphere by human activity since 1850 has remained in the atmosphere.

ATMOSPHERIC CHANGES

The greenhouse effect and the ozone hole are separate but related problems. For example, chlorofluorocarbons (CFCs) not only destroy stratospheric ozone but are also greenhouse gases.

CARBON TALLY

About 40 percent of the carbon added to the atmosphere by human activity since 1850 has remained in the atmosphere. The remaining 60 percent has been absorbed by the oceans and the terrestrial biosphere.

NATURAL RESPIRATION

A human being exhales 2.2 pounds of carbon dioxide per day.

MULTIPLIER EFFECT

Burning one gallon of gasoline, which weighs 6.3 pounds, produces 19.6 pounds of carbon dioxide because combustion links atmospheric oxygen to the carbon in the gasoline.

NOBEL ORACLE

The first person to predict that carbon dioxide released by burning fossil fuels would cause global warming was Swedish chemist and Nobel laureate Svante Arrhenius. He published a paper titled "On the influence of Carbonic Acid in the Air Upon the Temperature of the Ground" in *Philosophical Magazine* in 1896.

Soaking Up CO_2

Klaus Lackner is a geophysicist at the Earth Institute at Columbia University and codeveloper of the synthetic tree, a device designed to remove carbon dioxide from the air. By Lackner's calculations, one synthetic tree could absorb 1,000 times more CO_2 than a living tree.

Brad Lemley: *How would the synthetic tree remove carbon dioxide from the air?*

Klaus Lackner: The device itself would look something like goalposts with venetian blinds. It would be equipped to use liquid sodium hydroxide, which converts to sodium carbonate as it pulls CO_2 from the wind stream.

How much could one tree remove?

The unit, which has a collection area of 50 meters by 60 meters, could gather 90,000 tons of CO_2 a year. That means one synthetic tree could handle an amount equivalent to the annual emissions of 15,000 cars.

How many of these synthetic trees worldwide would be needed to soak up the 22 billion tons of CO_2 produced annually from fossil fuels?

About 250,000.

To make this process efficient, you need to recycle the sodium hydroxide, which means you need to take the absorbed carbon back out. How do you do that?

You percolate the liquid sodium carbonate over solid calcium hydroxide, and the calcium catches the carbon. So you have taken the carbon out of your sodium hydroxide, and you can use it again. But then you have to get the carbon out of the calcium so that you can repeat the process. You do this by heating the calcium carbonate to 900 degrees Celsius, and it lets loose the CO_2. So now we have the CO_2 back in hand as a concentrated stream, with which we can do whatever we want.

What do you suggest?

It can be sequestered underground. The question is, is there enough capacity? Short term, it will work, but for the long term we need to develop other alternatives. I have proposed mineral sequestration. There are entire mountain ranges made of magnesium silicates that over millions of years would naturally turn into magnesium carbonate. We could speed up that process in an industrial fashion. We could make a stable, harmless solid.

What percentage of the energy in, say, gasoline would be consumed in the process of cleaning it up?

About 40 percent. People say 40 percent is a big hit. But it's not, compared with producing hydrogen from coal, which I think is the most likely way large quantities of hydrogen would be made. Those guys also have a 40 percent energy hit, if not larger. So in a sense, the cleanup will cost that much, whether it is converting hydrogen from coal or pulling carbon dioxide from the air. In one case, you pay for the energy upstream; in the other you pay for it downstream.

Organizations to Contact

The editors have compiled the following list of organizations concerned with the issues debated in this book. The descriptions are derived from materials provided by the organizations. All have publications or information available for interested readers. The list was compiled on the date of publication of the present volume; the information provided here may change. Be aware that many organizations take several weeks or longer to respond to inquiries, so allow as much time as possible.

American Council on Science and Health (ACSH)
1995 Broadway, 2nd Floor, New York, NY   10023-5860
(212) 362-7044 • Fax: (212) 362-4919
E-mail: acsh@acsh.org
Web site: www.acsh.org

ACSH is a consumer education consortium concerned with environmental and health-related issues. The council publishes the quarterly *Priorities*, position papers such as "Global Climate Change and Human Health," and numerous reports, including *Arsenic, Drinking Water, and Health* and *The DDT Ban Turns 30.*

Canadian Centre for Pollution Prevention (C2P2)
215 Spadina Ave, Suite 134, Toronto, ON
  M5T 2C7
(800) 667-9790 • Fax: (416) 979-3936
E-mail: info@c2p2online.com
Web site: www.c2p2online.com

The Canadian Centre for Pollution Prevention is Canada's leading resource on ways to end pollution. It provides access to national and international information on pollution and prevention, online forums, and publications, including *Practical Pollution Training Guide* and the newsletter *At the Source,* which C2P2 publishes three times a year.

Cato Institute

1000 Massachusetts Ave. NW, Washington, D.C.   20001-5403
(202) 842-0200 • Fax: (202) 842-3490
E-mail: cato@cato.org
Web site: www.cato.org

The Cato Institute is a libertarian public policy research foundation that aims to limit the role of government and protect civil liberties. The institute believes EPA regulations are too stringent. Publications offered on the Web site include the bimonthly *Cato Policy Report*, the quarterly journal *Regulation*, the paper "The EPA's Clear Air-ogance," and the book *Climate of Fear: Why We Shouldn't Worry About Global Warming*.

Competitive Enterprise Institute (CEI)

1001 Connecticut Ave. NW, Suite 1250
Washington, D.C.   20036
(202) 331-1010 • Fax: (202) 331-0640
E-mail: info@cei.org
Web site: www.cei.org

CEI is a nonprofit public policy organization dedicated to the principles of free enterprise and limited government. The institute believes private incentives and property rights, rather than government regulations, are the best way to protect the environment. CEI's publications include the newsletter *Monthly Planet* (formerly *CEI Update*), *On Point* policy briefs, and the books *Global Warming and Other Eco-Myths* and *The True State of the Planet*.

Environment Canada

351 St. Joseph Boulevard, Gatineau, Quebec   K1A 0H3
   Canada
(819) 997-2800 • Fax: (819) 953-2225
E-mail: enviroinfo@ec.gc.ca
Web site: www.ec.gc.ca

Environment Canada is a department of the Canadian government. Its goal is the achievement of sustainable development in Canada through conservation and environmental protection. The department publishes reports, including the *Severe Weather Watcher Handbook*, and fact sheets on a number of topics, such as acid rain and pollution prevention.

Environmental Protection Agency (EPA)
Ariel Rios Building, 1200 Pennsylvania Avenue, NW
Washington, D.C. 20460
(202) 272-0167
Web site: www.epa.gov

The EPA is the federal agency in charge of protecting the environment and controlling pollution. The agency works toward these goals by enacting and enforcing regulations, identifying and fining polluters, assisting businesses and local environmental agencies, and cleaning up polluted sites. The EPA publishes periodic reports and the monthly *EPA Activities Update*.

Foundation for Clean Air Progress (FCAP)
601 Pennsylvania Avenue, N.W., North Building, Suite 540
Washington, D.C. 20004
Web site: www.cleanairprogress.org

FCAP is a nonprofit organization that believes the public is unaware of the progress that has been made in reducing air pollution. The foundation represents various sectors of business and industry in providing information to the public about improving air quality trends. FCAP publishes reports and studies demonstrating that air pollution is on the decline, including *Breathing Easier About Energy—A Healthy Economy and Healthier Air* and *Study on Air Quality Trends, 1970–2015*.

Friends of the Earth
1717 Massachusetts Avenue, NW, 600
Washington, D.C. 20036-2002
(877) 843-8687 • Fax: (202) 783-0444
E-mail: foe@foe.org

Friends of the Earth is dedicated to protecting the planet from environmental disaster and to preserving biological diversity. The organization encourages toxic waste cleanup and promotes the use of tax dollars to protect the environment. Its publications include the bimonthly newsletter *Environmental Roundup* and the books *Crude Awakening: The Oil Mess in America: Wasting Energy, Jobs, and The Environment;* and *Earth Budget: Making Our Tax Dollars Work for the Environment.*

Greenpeace U.S.A.
702 H Street, NW, Washington, D.C.   20001
(202) 462-1177 • Fax: (202) 462-4507
E-mail: greenpeace@wD.C..greenpeace.org
Web site: www.greenpeace.org/usa

Greenpeace opposes nuclear energy and the use of toxic chemicals and supports ocean and wildlife preservation. It uses controversial direct-action techniques and strives for media coverage of its actions in an effort to educate the public. It publishes the quarterly magazine *Greenpeace* and the books *Radiation and Health, Coastline,* and *The Greenpeace Book on Antarctica.*

The Heritage Foundation
214 Massachusetts Ave. NE, Washington, D.C.   20002
202.546.4400 • Fax: 202.546.8328
Web site: www.heritage.org

The Heritage Foundation is a conservative think tank that supports the principles of free enterprise and limited government in environmental matters. Its many publications include the quarterly magazine *Policy Review* and the occasional papers series "Heritage Talking Points," which periodically includes studies on environmental regulations and government policies.

Hudson Institute, Inc.
1015 15th Street, N.W. 6th Floor, Washington, D.C.   20005
202.974.2400 • Fax: 202.974.2410
Web site: www.hudson.org

The Hudson Institute is a public policy research center staffed by members elected from academia, government, and industry. The institute promotes free-market principles in the solution of environmental problems. Its publications include briefing papers such as "The Organic Farming Threat to People and Wildlife," which documents the problems of reducing pesticide use; books on education and the workforce; and newsletters such as *Global Food Quarterly*, which explores issues relating to agriculture and minorities.

National Resources Defense Council (NRDC)
40 W. 20th Street, New York, NY 10011
(212) 727-2700 • Fax: (212) 727-1773
E-mail: nrdcinfo@nrdc.org
Web site: www.nrdc.org

The NRDC is a nonprofit organization with more than four hundred thousand members. It uses laws and science to protect the environment, including wildlife and wild places. NRDC publishes *NRDC Online* and hundred of reports, including *Development and Dollars* and the annual report *Testing the Waters*.

Pew Center on Global Climate Change
2101 Wilson Blvd., Suite 550, Arlington, VA 22201
(703) 516-4146 • Fax: (703) 841-1422
Web site: www.pewclimate.org

The Pew Center is a nonpartisan organization dedicated to educating the public and policy makers about the causes and potential consequences of global climate change and informing them of ways to reduce the emissions of greenhouse gases. Its reports include *Designing a Climate-Friendly Energy Policy* and *The Science of Climate Change*.

Political Economy Research Center (PERC)
2048 Analysis Drive, Suite A, Bozeman, MT 59718
(406) 587-9591
E-mail: perc@perc.org
Web site: www.perc.org

PERC is a nonprofit research and educational organization that seeks market-oriented solutions to environmental problems. The center holds a variety of conferences and provides environmental educational material. It publishes the quarterly newsletter *PERC Reports*, commentaries, research studies, and policy papers, among them *Economic Growth and the State of Humanity* and *The National Forests: For Whom and For What?*

Sierra Club

85 Second Street, 2nd Floor, San Francisco, CA   94105-3441
(415) 977-5500 • Fax: (415) 977-5799
E-mail: information@sierraclub.org
Web site: www.sierraclub.org

The Sierra Club is a grassroots organization with chapters in every state that promotes the protection and conservation of natural resources. The organization maintains separate committees on air quality, global environment, and solid waste, among other environmental concerns, to help achieve its goals. It publishes books, fact sheets, the bimonthly magazine *Sierra* and the *Planet* newsletter, which appears several times a year.

Union of Concerned Scientists (UCS)

2 Brattle Square, Cambridge, MA   02238-9105
(617) 547-5552 • Fax: (617) 864-9405
E-mail: ucs@ucsusa.org
Web site: www.ucsusa.org

UCS aims to advance responsible public policy in areas where science and technology play important roles. Its programs emphasize transportation reform, arms control, safe and renewable energy technologies, and sustainable agriculture. UCS publications include the twice-yearly magazine *Catalyst*, the quarterly newsletter *Earthwise*, and the reports *Greener SUVs* and *Greenhouse Crisis: The American Response*.

Worldwatch Institute

1776 Massachusetts Ave. NW, Washington, D.C.   20036-1904
(202) 452-1999 • Fax: (202) 296-7365
E-mail: worldwatch@worldwatch.org
Web site: www.worldwatch.org

Worldwatch is a nonprofit public policy research organization dedicated to informing the public and policy makers about emerging global problems and trends and the complex links between the environment and the world economy. Its publications include *Vital Signs*, issued every year, the bimonthly magazine *World Watch*, the Environmental Alert series, and numerous policy papers, including *Unnatural Disasters* and *City Limits: Putting the Brakes on Sprawl.*

Bibliography

Books

William R. Cline	*Global Warming and Agriculture: Impact Estimates By Countries.* Washington, DC: Peterson Institute, 2007.
Al Gore	*The Assault on Reason.* New York: Penguin, 2008.
Al Gore	*The Inconvenient Truth: The Crisis of Global Warming.* New York: Viking, 2007.
Christopher C. Horner	*The Politically Incorrect Guide to Global Warming (and Environmentalism).* Washington, DC: Regnery, 2007.
John Houghton	*Global Warming: The Complete Briefing.* New York: Cambridge University Press, 2004.
Jeffrey Langholz and Kelly Turner	*You Can Prevent Global Warming (and Save Money!): 51 Easy Ways.* Kansas City, MO: Andrews McMeel, 2008.
Mark Maslin	*Global Warming: A Very Short Introduction.* New York: Oxford University Press, 2005.
Elizabeth May and Zoe Caron	*Global Warming for Dummies.* Hoboken, NJ: For Dummies, 2008.

Bill McKibben — *Fight Global Warming Now: The Handbook for Taking Action in Your Community.* New York: Holt, 2007.

Chris Mooney — *Storm World: Hurricanes, Politics, and the Battle over Global Warming.* New York: Harcourt, 2007.

S. George Philander — *Is the Temperature Rising? The Uncertain Science of Global Warming.* Princeton, New Jersey: Princeton University Press, 2000.

David de Rothschild — *The Live Earth Global Warming Survival Handbook: 77 Essential Skills to Stop Climate Change.* New York: Rodale, 2007.

Bernard F. Shulk — *Greenhouse Gases and Their Impact.* Hauppauge, NY: Nova Science, 2006.

S. Fred Singer — *Unstoppable Global Warming: Every 1500 Years.* New York: Rowman & Littlefield, 2008.

Debbie Stowell — *Climate Trading: Development of Greenhouse Gas Markets.* New York: Palgrave Macmillan, 2005.

Michael Tennesen — *The Complete Idiot's Guide to Global Warming,* 2nd edition, New York: Alpha, 2008.

Ernesto Zedillo — *Global Warming: Looking Beyond Kyoto.* Washington, DC: Brookings Institute, 2007.

Periodicals

William B.
Cassidy
"Alarming Increase in Expected Growth of China's CO2 Emissions," *Space Daily*, March 11, 2008.

"Trucking's Green Horizon," *Traffic World*, March 10, 2008.

Robert Colman
"Climate Challenge Pushes Law Officers to Go Green," *Legal Intelligencer*, February 29, 2008.

"The Climate Debate," *Oil and Gas Journal*, January 20, 2003.

"Corporate Social Responsibility—Taking the Lead," *CMB Management*, February 2005.

Daniel Fisher
"Current Affairs: Gaining Heat," *Pensions Week*, March 3, 2008.

"A Dirty Game," *Forbes*, March 10, 2008.

Daniel Fisher
"Selling the Blue Sky," *Forbes*, February 25, 2008.

Steve Forbes
"Brrr!" (Rising Temperatures and Starbucks Corp. Discontinues Some of Its Services), *Forbes*, March 10, 2008.

Deborah Gangloff
"Fighting Global Warming," *American Forests*, Summer 2007.

Melanie Haiken
"Dumping Iron," *Mother Jones*, March–April 2008.

Jeremy Jacquot   "Buried in the Sandstone Sponge: Fighting Global Warming By Storing CO_2 Just Got More Feasible," *Discover*, March 2008.

Shawn Rhea   "King Coal," *America*, March 3, 2008.

"Kyoto, Internationalism and Sovereignty," *Canadian Dimension*, November–December 2002.

"Money Meets Mouth: Green View," *Global Agenda*, February 25, 2008.

"Nitrous Oxide: Definitely No Laughing Matter," *Space Daily*, February 19, 2008.

"Greening the Supply Chain: Systems Find They Can Be Good to the Planet as Well as Their Bottom Line," *Modern Healthcare*, February 25, 2008.

Alex Scott   "Green Chemistry: Seeking New Routes to Tackle Emissions," *Chemical Week*, February 25, 2008.

Alex Steffen   "Cities: A Smart Alternative to Cars," *Business Week*, February 12, 2008.

Harry Stoffer   "Next President May Be Tougher on Industry," *Automotive News*, February 11, 2008.

Marc Wieder   "Tracking Your Carbon Footprint,"
                     Space Daily, February 26, 2008.

                     "Green Building Can Benefit Every-
                     one Involved," *Real Estate Weekly*,
                     February 27, 2008.

Ernesto Zedillo   "Carbon Prices, Not Quotas," *Forbes*,
                     March 24, 2008.

Index